FUSS-FREE FOOD FOR BABIES & TODDLERS
150 HEALTHY HOME-MADE RECIPES

FUSS-FREE FOOD FOR BABIES & TODDLERS

150 HEALTHY HOME-MADE RECIPES

Nutritious, delicious and easy-to-prepare dishes to give your baby and child a healthy start in life, shown step by step in 900 beautiful photographs

SARA LEWIS

LORENZ BOOKS

Dedication: To my children, William, aged 1, who has eaten every recipe in the book with great enthusiasm, and Alice, aged 5, the fussiest of fussy eaters.

This edition published by Lorenz Books

Lorenz Books is an imprint of Anness Publishing Limited
Hermes House, 88–89 Blackfriars Road, London SE1 8HA
tel. 020 7401 2077; fax 020 7633 9499

www.lorenzbooks.com; www.annesspublishing.com

If you like the images in this book and would like to investigate using them for publishing, promotions or advertising, please visit our website www.practicalpictures.com for more information.

UK agent: The Manning Partnership Ltd;
tel. 01225 478444; fax 01225 478440; sales@manning-partnership.co.uk
UK distributor: Grantham Book Services Ltd;
tel. 01476 541080; fax 01476 541061; orders@gbs.tbs-ltd.co.uk
North American agent/distributor: National Book Network;
tel. 301 459 3366; fax 301 429 5746; www.nbnbooks.com
Australian agent/distributor: Pan Macmillan Australia;
tel. 1300 135 113; fax 1300 135 103; customer.service@macmillan.com.au
New Zealand agent/distributor: David Bateman Ltd; tel. (09) 415 7664; fax (09) 415 8892

Publisher: Joanna Lorenz
Editorial Director: Judith Simons
Project Editors: Emma Wish and Molly Perham
Designer: Sue Storey
Special Photography: John Freeman
Stylist: Judy Williams
Home Economists: Sara Lewis, Jacqueline Clarke
and Petra Jackson

ETHICAL TRADING POLICY
Because of our ongoing ecological investment programme, you, as
our customer, can have the pleasure and reassurance of knowing
that a tree is being cultivated on your behalf to naturally
replace the materials used to make the book you are holding.
For further information about this scheme,
go to www.annesspublishing.com/trees

© Anness Publishing Limited 1995, 2007

Updated 2006

A CIP catalogue record for this book is available from the British Library.

ACKNOWLEDGEMENTS
• I am particularly grateful to the Department of
Health for reading and approving the section on
food for babies.
• National Dairy Council Nutrition Service
• Healthy Education Authority
• Dr Nigel Dickie from Heinz Baby Foods
• The British Dietetic Association
• The Health Visitors Association
• For Broadstone Communications for their
invaluable help supplying Kenward equipment for
recipe testing and photography
• Hand-painted china plates, bowls and mugs
from Cosmo Place Studio
• Tupperware for plain-coloured plastic bowls,
plates, feeder beakers and cups
• Cole and Mason for children's ware
• Royal Doulton for Bunnykins china
• Spode for blue and white Edwardian
Childhood china.

NOTES
• Bracketed terms are intended for American readers.
• For all recipes, quantities are given in both metric
and imperial measures and, where appropriate, in
standard cups and spoons. Follow one set, but not a
mixture, because they are not interchangeable.
• Standard spoon and cup measures are level.
1 tsp = 5ml, 1 tbsp = 15ml, 1 cup = 250ml/8fl oz.
• Australian standard tablespoons are 20ml.
Australian readers should use 3 tsp in place of
1 tbsp for measuring small quantities of gelatine,
flour, salt, etc.
• American pints are 16fl oz/2 cups. American
readers should use 20fl oz/2.5 cups in place of 1 pint
when measuring liquids.
• Electric oven temperatures in this book are for
conventional ovens. When using a fan oven, the
temperature will probably need to be reduced by
about 10–20°C/20–40°F. Since ovens vary, you
should check with your manufacturer's instruction
book for guidance.
• Medium (US large) eggs are used unless
otherwise stated.

PICTURE CREDITS
Bubbles: pages 87 br (Jacqui Farrow); pages
27 t, 41, 67 tr, 170 b, 173 t (Lois Joy Thurston);
page 31 t (F Rombout); page 75 (S Price); pages
86 t, 91 t (Ian West); page 171 t (Nikki Gibbs).

Lupe Cunha: pages 32, 38/39, 44, 47 t, 58,
73, 170 t.

Greg Evans: page 80.

Sally and Richard Greenhill: page 64 t.

Lyons Waddell: page 61 t.

Reflections/Jennie Woodcock: pages 65 b,
66 tr, 76/77, 79, 87 cr, 97, 126, 171 b, 172 bl br.

Timothy Woodcock: page 173.

Previously published as *Cooking for Babies & Toddlers*

CONTENTS

INTRODUCTION

Although during the first few years of any baby's life, food, diet and nutrition are vitally important to build a healthy and energetic child and to develop good eating habits that will see the infant safely through childhood, there is a real shortage of reliable, practical information on the subject.

This book aims to outline all you need to know about feeding your baby and toddler in one volume. Set out in three easy-to-use sections, the book is packed with over 200 recipes, all beautifully illustrated with colour pictures – from first purées, to tempting toddler meals, then moving on to food for all the family.

In the very early days all a baby needs is milk, but as it grows so too will its nutritional needs. By six months most babies will have doubled their birth weight and will be ready to begin mini-mouthfuls of simple mashed food.

Although this marks an exciting time in your baby's development, it can also cause immense worry for a new parent. We all want to provide the best for our child, and what better start in life is there than to begin laying down the foundations for a healthy diet? But what do you do if your child won't eat, or just spits out those delicious spoonfuls of food that you have so lovingly prepared? You will find practical, down-to-earth advice for coping with this and other problems, such as how to fit your baby's feeding schedule into daily life without causing major disruption to other members of the family.

FIRST FOODS
Section one covers everything you need to know about introducing those first few spoonfuls of smooth mashed or puréed foods, such as when to begin weaning, the signs to look out for that your baby is ready, which foods to serve and when, and which foods to avoid. It also includes invaluable advice on basic equipment, plus nutritional information, helpful guidelines on food preparation and masses of colourful and exciting recipes with which to tempt your baby.

Below: *Eating together as a family is important, and it is possible to produce separate meals for a baby, a toddler and the parents from one set of ingredients.*

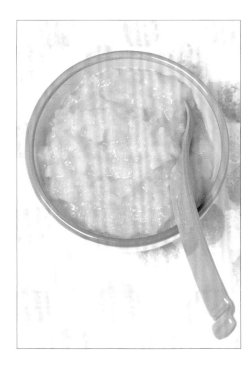

You will almost certainly find that helpful friends, relatives, health professionals and magazines will offer you differing and sometimes contradictory advice. Some will be genuinely useful, while some will be outdated or inappropriate: the difficulty is sorting through the well-meaning confusion to find something that is reliable. This book is based on the latest government information and advice, and aims to offer helpful advice in accordance with those guidelines.

FOOD FOR TODDLERS
In the second section we move on to feeding an energetic toddler. By this stage your baby will probably have tripled its birth weight and will have begun to feed itself, and may be developing strong likes and dislikes. Many young children go through a stage of extreme eating habits or food fads, causing immense frustration and worry for parents. Again we have included down-to-earth tips and practical advice on coping with a fussy eater. There are lots of easy and approachable recipes to tempt your child, while still providing a balanced and varied diet.

Above and left: *Throughout the book you will find advice and guidance on how to overcome fads and reluctance to eat – including hundreds of exciting and fun ideas to make meals more tempting and palatable for infants and toddlers of all ages.*

FAMILY MEALS
In the third section, the recipes have been devised to feed the whole family from one basic set of ingredients prepared at the same time. With step-by-step instructions we illustrate how to mash food for your baby, make a mini-meal for a fussy toddler and how, by just adding a few extra ingredients, to simultaneously transform this simple meal into something more exciting for adults.

Above and below: *Start with simple vegetable purées. Sit your baby in a high-chair with a strap, or on your lap with a dish towel to protect your clothes.*

FOOD AND YOUR CHILD

Childrens' nutritional needs are very different from our own. Forget about low-fat, high-fibre diets. Young children require nutrient-dense foods to meet their rapid levels of growth. Requirements for protein and energy are high in proportion to the child's size. Tiny tummies mean children are unable to eat large quantities of food, while at the same time they are usually very active. Their appetites can vary enormously, but the range of foods that they will eat may be very limited. Consequently, it is vital that the foods which are eaten contain a variety of nutrients, in combination with calories, while still fitting in with family meals. High-fibre foods can be very filling without providing sufficient levels of protein, vitamins and minerals.

For young infants fat is the major source of dietary energy: both breast milk and infant formula contribute about 50 per cent of energy as fat. As your child progresses to a mixed diet, the proportion of energy supplied by fat decreases and is replaced by carbohydrate. However, it is important that the energy is provided by fat up to the age of two, as too much carbohydrate may be too bulky for a young infant.

Adequate energy is necessary to sustain growth. Fat is a very useful source of energy and the main source of the fat-soluble vitamins, A, D, E and K, while also providing essential fatty acids that the body cannot make itself. It is best to obtain fat from foods that contain other essential nutrients, such as full-fat (whole) milk, cheese, yogurt, lean meat and small quantities of oily fish.

Try to include a portion of carbohydrate in every meal once your child is over nine months: for example, bread, potatoes, rice or pasta for energy. Encourage young

Below: *Babies are easily encouraged to take pleasure in their food, however simple. Give your baby finger food as well as a spoon and bowl.*

children to eat a variety of fruit and vegetables. As with adults, try to keep salt intakes to a minimum; fried foods or very sugary foods should be discouraged and served only as a special treat. As children approach school age they should gradually be pushed towards a diet that is lower in fat and higher in fibre, in line with the guidelines for adults.

Snacks are also important as young children require high calorie levels and cannot meet this requirement in three meals a day. Try to encourage healthy snacks such as mini ham sandwiches, cubes of cheese or wedges of apple instead of chocolate biscuits.

Obviously, having a healthy, well-balanced diet is essential for any age group, but acquiring social skills is also important. Our children learn from us and so it is vital to eat together as a family, if not every day, then as often as possible. It is never too early for the youngest member of the family to start learning how to behave at the table – though to begin with it will probably be a messy experience. Your child will soon regard family meals as a sociable and enjoyable time.

We hope that this book will make meal times fun for the entire family and help to minimize any problems you may come up against when feeding your baby and toddler.

Below: *Don't deprive the children of cakes at party-time, but include some healthy dips and savouries, too.*

Above: *Giving your child the best possible start in life is a major concern, but good food planning is easy to achieve.*

FIRST FOODS

Introducing your baby to the delights of solid food heralds the beginning of a new and exciting stage in your baby's development. You will know she is ready when she seems unsatisfied after a milk feed, or shows an interest in what you are eating. Although it will be a few months yet before she is able to share in family meals fully, the foods that you give your baby now are important not only for their nutritional benefits but also in laying down the first foundations for a healthy diet through childhood and beyond.

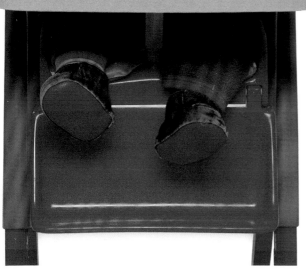

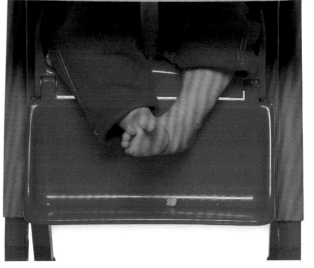

Start your baby with baby rice that is barely warm and only slightly thicker than milk – then move to bland mashed vegetables and fruits. For those first spoonfuls, sit your baby on your lap in a familiar position, but once she is accustomed to the idea, put her in a baby chair on the floor, or in a portable car seat. It won't be long before she is ready for a high-chair. Remember that hygiene is still very important, and you should continue to sterilize equipment until your baby is six-and-a-half months old.

Weaning from Milk Feeds to Solids

Most babies are ready to begin those first few mini-mouthfuls of mashed or puréed foods at around six months and will soon progress to a mixed diet of solid foods. By this age, babies need the extra energy, protein, iron and other essential nutrients that are found in solids in order to help them develop and grow. Your baby will also be progressing from sucking to biting and chewing – as many breast-feeding mothers find out!

Remember that every baby has individual needs, so don't be surprised if your baby seems ready for solids a little earlier or later than other babies of the same age. Don't feel pressurized by friends with young babies, or helpful relatives. Be guided by your own baby.

Below: Your baby will very quickly take an interest in your hand and the spoon, and will play as she eats.

Right: When the signs are right, start your baby with a few mouthfuls of mashed vegetables or fruit after a milk feed, or in the middle of one, if this works better. If the food is hot, make sure you stir it and test it before giving it to your baby.

Below right: When your baby starts picking up food and putting it into his mouth, he is ready to try solid foods.

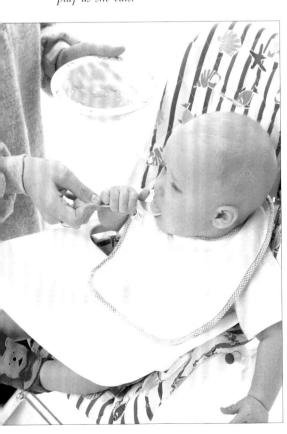

WHAT TO LOOK OUT FOR

If your baby:
- still seems hungry after you have increased the milk feed
- wants feeding more frequently
- shows a real interest in the foods that you are eating
- picks up food and puts it in his or her mouth, wanting to chew
- can sit up

If your baby is showing some or all of these signs, then he or she is probably ready to begin solids. Some babies may show these signs earlier than six months, but the majority should not be given solid foods before six months as their digestive systems can't cope. Be guided as well by any family history of allergies, eczema or asthma. Studies suggest that babies fed on breast or formula milk a bit longer are less likely to develop such complaints.

In the early days of weaning, your baby is not dependent on solid food for the supply of nutrients as this is still met by milk feeds. Don't worry if she only takes a taste of food to begin with – the actual experience of taking food off a spoon is the most important thing at this stage. However, as your baby grows older, solid foods are essential for supplying all the vital minerals and vitamins she needs.

WHAT ABOUT MILK FEEDS?

During the early stages of weaning, solids are given in addition to normal feeds of breast or formula milk. As mixed feeding continues, your baby will naturally cut down on the number of milk feeds, but milk will remain an important part of a child's diet.

Up to six months your baby should be having four to five milk feeds a day, and by age one your baby needs at least 600ml/1 pint full-fat (whole) milk a day. Milk will still contribute 40 percent of the energy she uses up. Health professionals recommend that children should not be given cow's milk as their main drink until after 12 months, due to low levels of iron and vitamins C and D. Mothers may be advised to go on to fortified formula when breast feeding has finished. Small amounts of cow's milk may be used in cooking from six months, but it is better to use formula milk.

Above: *Every baby is different. There is no need to be worried if your baby seems ready for solids earlier or later than other babies.*

Full-fat cow's milk can be given to children between one and two, while semi-skimmed (low-fat) milk can be gradually introduced to those over two,providing the child eats well. Skimmed milk should not be given to children under five.

Only give pasteurized milk to children. UHT or long-life milk is a useful standby for holidays and travelling as it doesn't need to be refrigerated. However, once opened treat it as full-fat pasteurized milk.

Some people prefer to give goat's or sheep's milk believing it is less allergenic and offers additional nourishment, although this cannot be substantiated. Goat's milk is deficient in folic acid and must not be given to babies under six months. Boil goat's milk before use, as it may be sold unpasteurized.

WEANING FROM BREAST OR BOTTLE

You can go on breast feeding your baby, as well as giving solid food, for as long as you wish. However, many mothers are quite relieved when their baby is happy to try a feeder

cup or bottle along with their lunch-time "solid" meal. Once solids become established the number of daytime milk feeds naturally tails off, with just the special morning and evening comfort feeds continuing until you and your baby are ready to stop.

Whether bottle or breast and bottle feeding, try to wean your baby off the bottle completely by the age of one. Otherwise your baby may find it difficult to give the bottle up, and comfort sucking on a teat can be a hard habit to break.

Once your baby can sit up, you can introduce a lidded feeding cup, initially at one meal a day, then at two and so on. But do make sure that you cuddle your baby while giving a drink, so that the baby still enjoys the closeness and security of being with her mother or father. There may be a few setbacks when your baby is teething or unwell, but be guided by your baby.

Above: *Bottles are a wonderful aid, but try to wean your baby off them by age one, or the sucking habit can be difficult to break.*

Above: *It won't all happen at once: a mixed period of feeding with breast, bottle and simple solids is perfectly natural and healthy.*

Introducing Solid Food

Many parents find that around late morning, after their baby's morning sleep, is the best time to introduce solids. The baby is happy and nicely hungry without being frantic. Offer a small milk feed to take the edge off her immediate hunger and make her feel secure, and then go on to offer solid food. Finish with the rest of the milk feed or "second side".

SITTING COMFORTABLY
If you are feeding a slightly younger baby, you might like to hold her securely on your lap while offering the first spoonfuls. However, most babies will be comfortable fed in a high-chair.

FIRST SPOONFULS
Baby rice is often the most successful first food because its milky taste and soft texture seem vaguely familiar to the baby. Begin by trying a teaspoonful of bought baby rice, add a little previously boiled water, expressed breast milk or formula milk as the pack directs, and mix to make a smooth runny purée, slightly thicker than milk. Test the temperature on the edge of your lip, it should be just lukewarm – too hot and you may put the baby off solids completely. Offer tiny amounts on the end of a sterilized teaspoon. Go at your baby's pace and don't try to hurry things.

Above: *First baby rice will be barely warm, and only very slightly thicker than milk.*

Learning to eat from a spoon is quite a skill, and your baby may start spitting out the food until she has mastered the technique of taking food off the spoon and transferring it to the back of her mouth. It is possible that she may not like the taste of the food. If you started with baby rice, then go on to potato or parsnip purée mixed into the baby rice. If your baby seems reluctant, then abandon the feed and go back to breast or bottle feeding – your baby may simply not be ready for solids yet.

You could try solids again a few days later – there's plenty of time. Never force-feed and never add solid foods to a baby's bottle, as it can lead to choking, which can be dangerous.

BABY APPEARS TO GAG
Some babies just cannot cope with solids at first and may seem distressed and almost gag on the food.

Above: *At about six months your baby will be ready to sit safely in a high-chair. You should always use a strap to make sure she is safely fastened in.*

Try thinning down the food even more, as it may be too thick. Alternatively, you may be putting too much on the spoon: try offering your baby a little less. If neither of these seems to help, stop solids and breast or bottle feed as usual, giving your baby plenty of reassuring cuddles. Try again in a few days' or weeks' time.

INTRODUCING VEGETABLES
After rice, gradually introduce mashed or puréed potato, carrot, parsnip and swede (rutabaga), or puréed apple or pears. As always, be guided by your baby: this is a slow process so don't try to hurry your baby if she is not ready, or you will run the risk of discouraging her altogether.

SPOON FEEDING FOR THE FIRST TIME

1 Sit your baby on your lap in a familiar position. Always test the temperature of the food.

2 Offer the spoon to your baby. Go slowly and if the spoon or food is rejected try again another day.

3 When your baby has taken her first solid food, sit her quietly for a little while in an upright position.

After a week or two your baby may be ready to try two mini-meals a day. Increase the amount of food to 10ml/2 tsp, even 15ml/3 tsp if your baby seems ready. You may be able to slightly reduce the amount of formula or breast milk you use to make the purée, so that it is not quite so sloppy. If your baby likes the flavour, then offer it again for a few meals before introducing a new taste. If your baby spits it out, then go back to baby rice or try mixing the new flavour with a little baby rice so that it is milder and more palatable.

Try to follow your baby's appetite and pace; most babies will stop when they have had enough. Don't be tempted to persuade your baby to finish off those last few spoonfuls. It's a bad habit to force or encourage anyone to clear the plate if they are full. If you do it with a baby, she'll probably be sick!

Adopt a feeding schedule to suit you both. In the early days it may be easier to give the baby breakfast before older children get up, or after they're at school, when the house is quieter. Six to eight weeks into solid feeding, your baby will probably be ready for three small meals a day. Again, be guided by her needs and appetite, so don't introduce a third meal until you feel she is really ready. Aim to feed your baby at roughly equal time intervals that will eventually coincide with as many family meals as possible.

TIPS

● Take advice from your doctor or health visitor, particularly if your baby was premature.

● Sterilize all equipment before use up to the age of about six-and-a-half months.

● Don't force your baby if she doesn't seem ready for solids – be guided by her and let it happen at its own pace.

● Maintain milk feeds and offer plain boiled water or very diluted fruit juice as well.

● Try one taste at a time and continue with this until your baby is accustomed to it. If she doesn't like it, don't offer it again for a few days.

● Allow plenty of time for feeding, particularly at first.

● Choose a time of day when you and your baby are relaxed.

● Talk to your baby quietly and encourage her to eat.

● Never leave your baby alone when feeding her.

● Remember, babies don't mind repetition – they've been living on milk for months!

Above: *You can build up the diet from baby rice to items like mashed or puréed carrot, parsnip, apple or pear, gradually leaving more texture as your baby seems ready.*

EQUIPMENT

Choose a small plastic spoon, preferably with a shallow bowl that is gentle on your baby's gums. Look out for packs of weaning spoons in pharmacies or baby-care shops. If you don't want to buy a lot of equipment right away, you may find it useful to mix small quantities of baby rice in the sterilized cap of a bottle. Alternatively, use a small china ramekin or plastic bowl. Plastic bowls with suction feet or insulated linings are also perfectly adequate and will be useful later on when your baby gets bigger. All equipment must be scrupulously clean (and sterilized if your baby is under six-and-a-half months old).

Below: This shallow bowl with a spoon would be the perfect starter set.

Above, left and below: Any small dish, or even the lid of a baby's bottle, can be used for mixing and feeding.

Below: A bib is even more essential once your baby is taking solid foods.

Left: A bowl with an insulated lining is a good idea for a baby who takes her time eating.

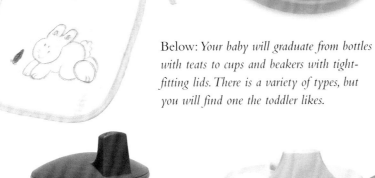

Below: Your baby will graduate from bottles with teats to cups and beakers with tight-fitting lids. There is a variety of types, but you will find one the toddler likes.

FEEDING TWINS

Probably the easiest way to feed twins is to sit the babies side by side and offer food from one bowl. Twins can get rather frustrated if you have to keep picking up different bowls and spoons. Try to be adaptable and if you find a way that works then stick with it. Encourage finger foods slightly earlier: perhaps a mini ham sandwich, cooked broccoli floret or carrot stick.

Wait until each child has finished their main course before offering dessert, as the slow eater will be distracted and want to go on to dessert too.

Looking after twins can be exhausting so you may find serving sandwiches for lunch an easier option, and this will give you a chance to eat something too. Serve cooked food for the evening meal.

DRINKS

Although your baby will need less milk for nourishment, she will still need something to drink, especially in hot weather. Always offer at least two drinks during the day and also a drink with every meal.

You can give:

- breast, formula milk or, at over one year, full-fat (whole) cow's milk
- cooled boiled water
- well-diluted pure unsweetened fruit juice

Above: *If you have twins, put their chairs side by side at meal-times.*

Below: *Drinks fill up the baby's tummy – so offer drinks after food.*

You can stop boiling the water for the baby's drinks when you stop sterilizing her feeding equipment, but always make sure you provide water from the mains supply and allow the tap to run before using it. Never use water from the hot tap.

If you have a water softener make sure that you use a tap connected directly to the mains supply and independent of the water softener. Artificially softened water is not recommended as salts are added during the softening process. Check with your doctor or health visitor before giving a baby bottled water, as the mineral content varies and you will need to choose a low-mineral brand such as those that are labelled "spring water". As a general rule, bottled water is not really necessary unless you are on holiday (vacation) where it is unsafe to drink the water.

Some fruit drinks contain a lot of added sugar, so check the label for sucrose, glucose, dextrose, fructose, maltose, syrup, honey or concentrated fruit juice. If you do give concentrated drinks to your baby, make sure you dilute them correctly, and do not give them too often. Pure fruit juices contain no

Above: *Dilute juices with boiled and cooled water.*

added sugar. At first, dilute them with one part juice to three parts water. The amount of water can be reduced as the child matures. Offer drinks at the end of meal times once your baby has settled into three meals a day.

Never allow a baby to use a bottle of juice as a comforter or go to sleep with a bottle in his mouth, as this can result in serious tooth decay.

Sterilizing and Food Preparation

For babies older than six months, it isn't necesssary for the first solids to be completely smooth and soft, and you can start introducing some texture quite quickly, depending on your baby's preferences. Fork-mashing is simple and easy, but there are several useful pieces of kitchen equipment to help you with larger quantities.

For ease and speed, an electric liquidizer is by far the best. You may be able to buy a liquidizer attachment for your mixer, or purchase a free-standing liquidizer unit. A food processor works well, but make sure the food is blended to the required smoothness before offering it to your baby, as processors can miss the odd lump, especially when processing small quantities. A hand-held electric multimixer has the bonus of reducing washing up by mixing foods in the serving bowl. If you prefer to purée food by hand, then a sieve (strainer) or hand mill are both perfectly adequate and are much cheaper alternatives.

Above: *There is a huge range of brand-name food processors and blenders on the market, many of which have attachments for puréeing.*

Left: *The basics – manual mashers, or a sieve – take longer but will do the job just as well.*

Above: *A purpose-designed liquidizer will make perfect purée in seconds. This is the right tool for making large batches.*

Above: *This hand-held blender takes a little longer, but the results are just as reliable. They are easy to clean and store.*

Above: *Making purée manually the old-fashioned way – with a sieve and spoon – is time-consuming but highly satisfying.*

FOOD HYGIENE

Young babies can easily pick up infections, so it is vitally important that all equipment is scrupulously clean before use.

• Always wash your hands before handling food or feeding equipment.

Above: *Rule one – always wash your hands with soap and warm water before feeding your baby or handling food.*

• Items such as bottles, feeding spoons and serving bowls should be sterilized until your baby is six-and-a-half months old. Sterilize equipment by boiling it in a pan of water for 25 minutes, immersing it in a container of cold water with sterilizing fluid or a tablet, or by using a steam sterilizer. Larger items such as a sieve, knife, pan, blender or masher, or plastic chopping board should be scalded with boiling water.

Above: *Scald larger objects such as chopping boards, spoons, sieves and pans with boiling water to sterilize.*

• Sterilize all baby equipment until your baby is six-and-a-half months; milk bottles, teats and so on should be sterilized until she begins to use a cup.

Above: *Boiling for 25 minutes is still the simplest way of sterilizing baby equipment.*

Right: *Always cover baby food at all times – even when stored in the refrigerator.*

Below: *Always keep the surfaces around where your baby eats scrupulously clean.*

• Never use equipment used for the family pet when preparing baby food. Keep a can opener, fork and dish specifically for your pet, and make sure other members of the family are aware of this.

• Once cooked, cover all baby food with a lid or plate and transfer to the refrigerator as soon as possible. Food should not be left for longer than 1½ hours at room temperature before either refrigerating or freezing.

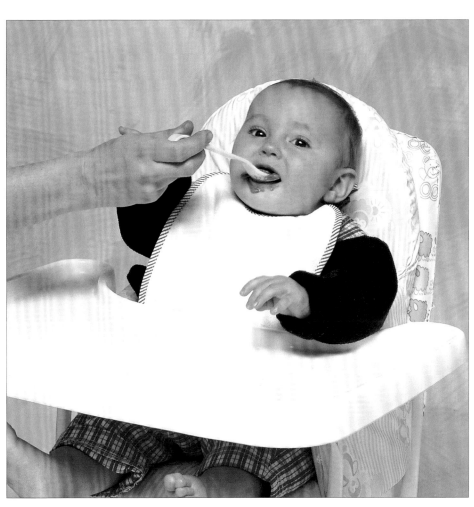

SOLUTION STERILIZER

1 Fill the sterilizer to the required height with cold water, and add sterilizing tablets or liquid.

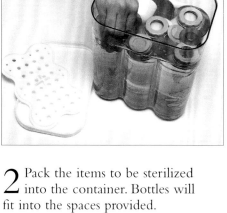

2 Pack the items to be sterilized into the container. Bottles will fit into the spaces provided.

STEAM STERILIZER

1 Measure the specified amount of water into the base of the steamer as directed in the instructions.

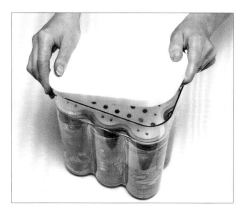

3 Make sure no air gets trapped in the container – or these pockets will not be properly sterile. Push everything down with the "float".

4 Place the lid on and leave for the length of time specified in the instructions. Rinse everything afterwards in boiling water.

2 Pack the bottles and teats into the container: steamers have less capacity for dishes, which will need to be boiled separately.

Left: *There is a wide range of sterilizing equipment to choose from. This group, all specially designed for bottles and teats, comprises two steam sterilizing units that operate electrically and a traditional container that holds the bottles efficiently in cold water sterilizing solution.*

STERILIZING IN THE MICROWAVE

Microwave ovens are not suitable for general day-to-day sterilizing without special equipment, and many health authorities and mother-and-baby experts recommend against using the microwave for this purpose. However, microwave sterilizing units can be purchased for sterilizing bottles, and if you are using one, the manufacturer's instructions should be followed closely.

Right: *This purpose-designed sterilizing unit is specially made for microwave use. Add about 5mm/¹/₄in water to the base before putting in the bottles.*

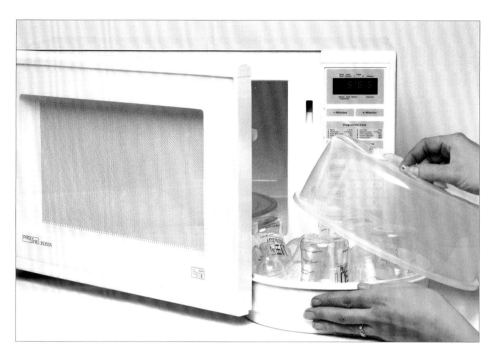

BATCH COOKING

Cooking for a baby can be very frustrating. Those spoonfuls of lovingly and hygienically prepared food, offered with such hope and spat out so unceremoniously can leave you feeling quite indignant.

Save time by cooking several meals in advance. Freeze mini-portions in ice-cube trays, great for those early days when you need only one cube for lunch, and flexible enough for later on when your baby's appetite has grown to two or three cubes per meal.

Spoon the mixture into sterilized ice-cube trays and open freeze until solid. Press the cubes into a plastic bag, seal, label and return to the freezer. Keep single batches of food in the same bag so that the different flavours don't combine.

Recycle yogurt containers, cottage cheese containers with lids, small plastic boxes with lids, or use disposable plastic cups and cover them with clear film (plastic wrap). Sterilize the containers using sterilizing fluid or tablets. Cover all prepared foods and label them clearly so that you know what they are and on which date they went into the freezer.

Most foods should be used within three months if stored in a freezer at – 18°C/0°F. Defrost plastic boxes in the refrigerator overnight. Ice cubes can be left to defrost at room temperature in a bowl or on a plate, loosely covered with clear film.

BATCH COOKING TIPS

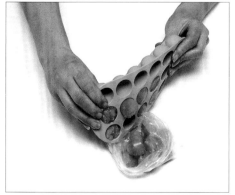

1 It is just as quick (and very much cheaper in the long run) to make a larger batch of purée as a smaller quantity for a single meal.

2 Freeze in meal-size portions in sterilized ice-cube trays: these can later be put into freezer bags for storing.

3 Make sure the bags are carefully labelled and dated. Keep only for the period specified in your freezer handbook.

Reheating, Freezing and Using a Microwave

HOW TO REHEAT BABY FOOD
Although reheating food sounds relatively straightforward, it is vitally important that the following rules are followed, as tepid food provides the perfect breeding ground for bacteria, especially if left uncovered in a warm kitchen and reheated several times.
● Don't reheat food more than once. It is a health risk, and can be dangerous.

● If you have a large batch of baby food, then reheat just a portion in a pan and leave the remaining mixture in a covered bowl in the refrigerator. If your baby is still hungry after the feed, then reheat a little extra again, with the remaining mixture left in the refrigerator.
● Reheat small quantities of baby food in a sterilized heat-proof container, covered with a saucer or

small plate and put into a small pan half filled with boiling water. Alternatively, spoon larger quantities straight into a pan, cover and bring to the boil.
● Make sure food is piping hot all the way through to kill any bacteria. Food should be 70°C/158°F for a minimum of 2 minutes. Take off the heat and allow to cool. Test before serving to your baby.

REHEATING TIPS

1 Reheat small quantities in a sterilized bowl, covered with a dish or foil.

2 Place the bowl into a pan half filled with boiling water. Make sure the food is cooked through.

3 For larger quantities, put the food straight into the pan and bring to the boil.

FREEZING

● When using a freezer for storing home-made baby foods, use up the foods as soon as possible, as the texture preferred by the child will change very quickly as she develops.
● Keeping a well-stocked freezer of basic provisions can be a life-saver: there is nothing worse than going shopping with small children, especially when they're tired, and freezing will save you trip after trip.
● Make sure to always label foods so you know exactly when they went into the freezer, and double check against this handy list of storage dates:

Meat and poultry

Beef and lamb	4–6 months
Pork and veal	4–6 months
Minced (ground) beef	3–4 months
Sausages	2–3 months
Ham and bacon joints	3–4 months
Chicken and turkey	10–12 months
Duck and goose	4–6 months

Fish

White fish	6–8 months
Oily fish	3–4 months
Fish portions	3–4 months
Shellfish	2–3 months

Fruit and vegetables

Fruit with or without sugar	8–10 months
Fruit juices	4–6 months
Most vegetables	10–12 months
Mushrooms and tomatoes	6–8 months

Dairy produce

Cream	6–8 months
Butter, unsalted (sweet)	6–8 months
Butter, salted	3–4 months
Cheese, hard	4–6 months
Cheese, soft	3–4 months
Ice cream	3–4 months

Prepared foods

Ready-prepared meals, highly seasoned	2–3 months
Ready-prepared meals, average seasoning	4–6 months
Cakes	4–6 months
Bread, all kinds	2–3 months
Other yeast products and pastries	3–4 months

Chart published by kind permission of the Food Safety Advisory Centre

Above: *Many parents will find a microwave helpful and time-saving if used carefully. It can be used for heating milk and drinks (for toddlers – not newborns), for defrosting, reheating and cooking preprepared foods.*

USING A MICROWAVE

Health advisers do not recommend using a microwave for reheating, as the food heats up unevenly, but if you decide to microwave baby food, then make sure you stir the food thoroughly after cooking. Leave the dish to stand for 2–3 minutes before stirring again so that "hot spots" are well stirred into the mixture, and always check the temperature before serving. Choose the type of dish carefully as some ceramic dishes can get very hot; plastic or pyrex dishes are the most successful in the microwave, heating food quickly but staying relatively cool themselves.

1 Cover with clear film (plastic wrap), pierce and place in the oven.

2 When cooked, remove from the microwave oven and stir.

MICROWAVING TIPS

● Never warm milk for a newborn or young baby in the microwave.

● For older children, warm milk in a bottle without the teat or in an uncovered feeder beaker for 30–45 seconds. Stir well and always test the temperature of the milk (*not* the temperature of the container) before serving to make sure that the milk is an even and comfortable temperature. Seek advice from your doctor or health visitor.

● To defrost ice cubes of baby food, press three into a baby dish, cover with clear film (plastic wrap) and thaw in the microwave on Defrost (30%) for 1–2 minutes. Stir well then re-cover and microwave on Full Power (100%) for 1 minute. Stir well to avoid hot spots, then test the temperature.

Choosing a High-chair

There is a surprisingly wide choice of high-chairs available in a range of finishes, colours and price levels, so make sure you shop around before you buy. Those shown here are just a selection of the many different chairs that are available.

Three-in-one-type

CONVERTIBLE CHAIRS

Designed for babies between four weeks and six months, these chairs can convert from a high-chair into a swing, and some models will also convert into a baby chair and rocker too. It is best to buy one of these when the baby is very young so that you get maximum use from it. The only disadvantage may be the space required for the frame. The ease in converting from one type of chair to another varies from model to model, so you would be well advised to practise in the shop before choosing which one to buy. Most chairs have white painted frames.

THREE-IN-ONE CHAIRS

Various designs on the market convert into a separate chair, chair and table or high-chair. Some simply clip apart, while others require a little help with a screwdriver. There are good rigid structures available with a wide range of decorative seat patterns. They are available in wood or white finishes. The low chair is suitable for children up to four years old if used without the tray.

ELEVATOR CHAIRS

These chairs are slightly more expensive, but will convert from a high-chair to a low chair. Some models have adjustable tray settings to fit a growing child. The frames are mostly available in white metal, with attractive seating.

Elevator type

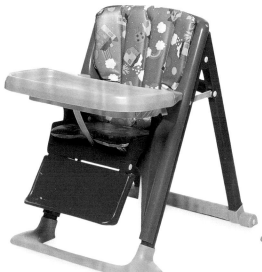

TIPS
• For maximum use of a high-chair, buy a booster cushion for the early days when your baby first begins to use the chair. Adjust the tray position as well, if possible.
• Check that the high-chair is easy to clean – dried-on food in cracks can be impossible to clean off. Look out for possible dirt traps on the seat or around the tray fixing.
• Make sure that the chair is sturdy and rigid – it will need to withstand considerable wear.

Above: *A portable clip-on chair.*

• If using a clip-on high-chair make sure that the table is suitable and will be able to withstand the weight of your child. Never, in any circumstances, fix on to glass.

FOLDING CHAIRS

These less expensive chairs, available in wood or white finishes, usually fold up in a scissor movement. Some can be folded crossways for packing into the boot (trunk) of the car. Before buying, check how easy they are to fold out and up, and make sure the frame is rigid when opened out.

Folding type

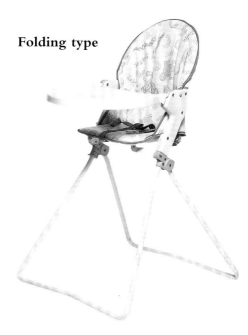

COUNTRY-TYPE CHAIRS

These are sturdy wooden high-chairs usually with a wooden tray and attractive spindle features. The seat can be hard for the baby, so it is best to buy a fitted chair cushion.

PORTABLE CHAIRS

There are two main types available:
● A very simple cloth tie, useful for visiting friends or eating out, as it will fold up and fit in a bag. However, it is not really suitable for everyday use as the child is literally tied on to the chair and so cannot reach the table to feed himself.
● Clip-on seats where the frames are placed under and over the edge of a dining table. Check that the table is strong enough and is not likely to overbalance before you put your baby in the chair.

1 Undo the tray catches by pressing both sides at once, and fold the tray upwards.

3 This allows you to fold the chair over on to itself: the design is incredibly neat and compact.

TIPS
● Always use a safety harness. Although most high-chairs have a three-point lap strap, you will probably have to buy straps that will go around your baby's body and clip on to the chair. It is amazing how quickly a baby learns to wriggle out of a high-chair when you're not looking.
● Never leave a child in a high-chair unattended.

2 Undo the side catches that keep the frame rigid so the chair can scissor in two.

4 It is now ready for storing, putting out of the way, or placing in the boot (trunk) of the car.

Above: *Always strap your baby in tightly.*

Going Vegetarian

A vegetarian diet can provide all the necessary nutrients for health and vitality, but it is important to balance the baby's diet to ensure that she receives adequate supplies of protein, vitamins D and B12, calcium and iron.

The basic guidelines are the same as for weaning any other baby: introduce flavours slowly and be guided by your baby. The biggest differences are obviously in the type of foods offered. Instead of obtaining protein from meat and fish, your baby will receive it from other protein-rich food. These include eggs, beans, peas, split lentils, and grains, finely ground nuts or nut creams, sunflower seed spread, milk and dairy products, and vegetarian cheese where available.

Vegetarians need to make sure that sufficient iron is included in their baby's diet. If she is over six months, offer prune juice, puréed apricots, molasses, refined lentils and cereals, particularly fortified breakfast cereals. Green vegetables and well-mashed beans, if over eight months, are also a good source of iron. Vitamin C aids the absorption of iron from plant sources, so make sure you serve fresh green vegetables or fruit in the meal. Your doctor may also think it is beneficial for your baby to take vitamin drops.

If you plan to bring the baby up as a vegan and so omit dairy products and eggs from the diet, then it is vital to consult your doctor or dietician.

Vegetarian diets tend to be bulky and lower in calories than a diet containing meat, so make sure you include foods that are protein and calorie rich, with little or no fibre, such as eggs, milk and cheese. These can be mixed with smaller quantities of vegetables, fruit and cereals. Fibre-rich foods can also be difficult for a child to digest as many nutrients

Above: *Raising your child as a vegetarian takes special planning and care to make sure all the necessary nutrients are included.*

may pass straight through the body. To ensure your baby is getting the correct amount of vitamins, minerals and food energy her diet should include foods from the four groups on the opposite page.

Oranges

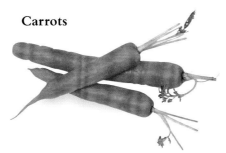

Carrots

Cucumber

Grapes

Cereals and grains: baby rice no earlier than 17 weeks; pasta, bread, oats and breakfast cereals from 7 months.

Fruit and vegetables: begin with potato, carrot, apple and pear at 6 to 6½ months, progressing to stronger-flavoured foods such as broccoli, beans, oranges and plums as your baby develops.

Dairy produce: including milk, cheese, fromage frais and yogurt from 7 months.
Note: Make sure cheese is rennet-free. If you are unsure, ask the delicatessen assistant, or check the packet if pre-packed.

Beans, peas and lentils: split and softly cooked lentils from 6–6½ months. Gradual introduction of tofu, smooth peanut butter, hard-boiled egg from 7 months. Well-cooked, mashed dried beans and peas and finely ground nuts from 9 months. Do not give whole nuts to the under-fives.

To make sure your baby is thriving and happy, irrespective of the type of diet, make sure you check your baby's weight at regular intervals at the health clinic.

Split peas

Lentils

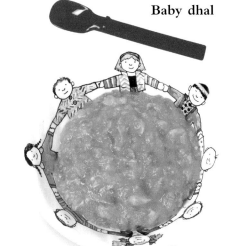

Baby dhal

STAGE 1: FIRST TASTES – EARLY WEANING

O FFICIAL GUIDELINES NOW RECOMMEND THAT WEANING TAKES PLACE AT SIX OR SIX–AND–A–HALF MONTHS, BUT THERE ARE SOME BABIES WHO SHOW INTEREST IN EATING SOLIDS AT AN EARLIER AGE. YOU SHOULD NOT INTRODUCE SOLID FOODS BEFORE YOUR BABY IS 17 WEEKS OLD – AND BE SURE TO ASK YOUR DOCTOR OR HEALTH VISITOR FOR ADVICE BEFORE STARTING EARLY WEANING. BEGIN BY OFFERING ONLY A TEASPOONFUL OF BABY RICE OR VERY SOFT RUNNY PURÉE ONCE A DAY. MILK IS STILL PROVIDING YOUR BABY WITH ALL HER NUTRITIONAL NEEDS, BUT THESE EARLY FOODS WILL BE THE FOUNDATIONS ON WHICH LATER EATING HABITS ARE BUILT, SO IT SHOULD BE A POSITIVE EXPERIENCE.

Suitable Foods

FOODS TO INCLUDE
- baby rice mixed with water, breast or formula milk
- mild-tasting fork-mashed vegetables – beginning with potato then carrot, parsnip, or swede (rutabaga)
- mild, naturally-sweet fruit purées made with eating apples or pears

Below: *If your baby seems ready to start taking solids at around four to five months old, start with a teaspoon and build gradually to two and finally three meals a day.*

Baby rice

Apple

Pear

Potato

Swede (rutabaga)

Carrot

Parsnip

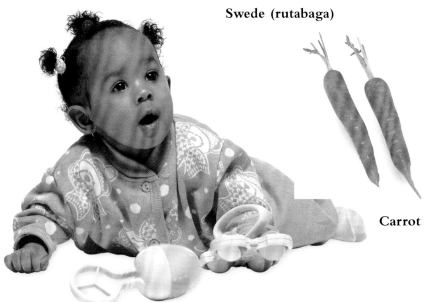

FOODS TO AVOID
- highly spiced foods
- salt as this causes the kidneys to overwork. Avoid seasoning with salt or adding stock cubes, bacon and salami to foods
- cows' milk (give breast or formula milk feeds instead)
- foods containing gluten, found in wheat, oats, rye and barley (check pack labels)
- eggs
- meat, fish, poultry
- citrus and berry fruits – can result in allergic reactions in some babies
- nuts, either whole or ground
- honey
- fatty foods

Right: Adult favourites – but these must be avoided at this age, even as treats.

Note: If you have a family history of allergies, your doctor or health visitor may also advise you to avoid other foods. Check with them.

Above: A world of foodstuffs opens up over the months: but introduce them gradually, and at the right time.

Baby Rice

Mix 5-15ml/1-3 tsp rice with cooled boiled water, formula or breast milk as the pack directs. Cool slightly and test before serving.

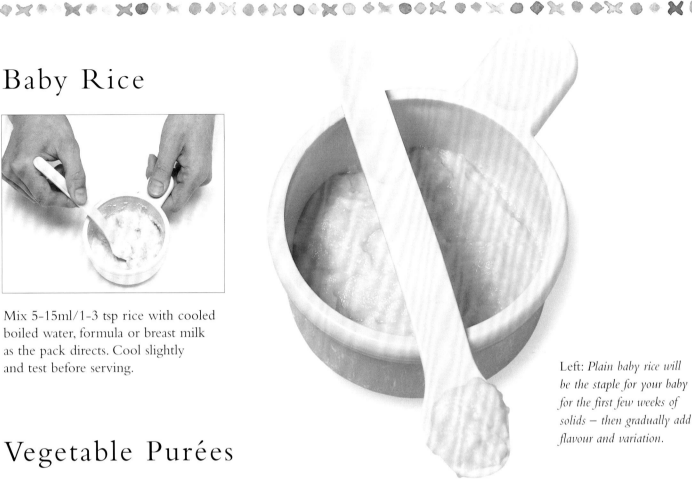

Left: *Plain baby rice will be the staple for your baby for the first few weeks of solids – then gradually add flavour and variation.*

Vegetable Purées

Makes: 175ml/6fl oz/¾ cup

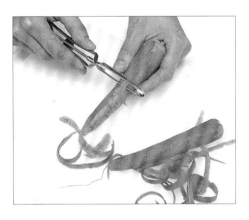

1 Peel 125g/3½oz potato, parsnip, carrot or swede (rutabaga) and chop into small dice.

● **To microwave**: put the vegetable or vegetables in a microwave-proof bowl with 30ml/2 tbsp formula or breast milk. Cover with clear film (plastic wrap), pierce and cook on Full Power (100%) for 4 minutes. Leave to stand for 5 minutes, then press through a sieve (strainer) and mix with 30–45ml/2–3 tbsp formula or breast milk. Cool and serve as above.

2 Steam over a pan of boiling water for 10 minutes, until soft.

3 Press through a sieve (strainer), mix with 60–75ml/4–5 tbsp formula or breast milk, depending on the vegetable used. Spoon a little into a bowl, test on a spoon and cool if needed. Cover the remaining purée and transfer to the refrigerator as soon as possible. Use within 24 hours.

Fruit Purées

Makes: 120ml/4fl oz/½ cup

1 Peel, quarter and core 1 dessert apple or 1 ripe pear.

2 Thinly slice and put in a small pan with 15ml/1 tbsp water, formula or breast milk. Cover and simmer for 10 minutes, until soft.

• **To microwave:** place the apple or pear in a microwave-proof bowl with water, formula or breast milk. Cover with clear film (plastic wrap), pierce and cook on Full Power (100%) for 3 minutes. Leave to stand for 5 minutes, then press through a sieve (strainer). Cool and serve as above.

3 Press through a sieve (strainer). Spoon a little purée into a serving bowl, test on a spoon and cool if needed. Cover, transfer to the refrigerator, and use within 24 hours.

Top: *Pear and apple purée (top) will bring a smile to any baby's face (above).*

STAGE 2: AROUND SIX TO SIX-AND-A-HALF MONTHS

IF YOU BEGIN WEANING AT SIX MONTHS, START WITH BABY RICE AND RUNNY VEGETABLE AND FRUIT PURÉE. IF YOU HAVE ALREADY INTRODUCED YOUR BABY TO SOLIDS, INCREASE THE VARIETY OF FOODS OFFERED AND START TO COMBINE FOOD TASTES. PURÉE CAN BE A THICKER COARSER TEXTURE, BUT MAKE SURE THERE ARE NO PIPS (SEEDS) OR BONES. ALWAYS CHOOSE THE BEST, FRESHEST INGREDIENTS AND MAKE SURE UTENSILS ARE SCRUPULOUSLY CLEAN.

Suitable Foods

FOODS TO INCLUDE
- wide selection of vegetables, including fresh or frozen peas, corn, cauliflower, broccoli, cabbage, spinach, celery, mushrooms and leeks
- fruits – banana, apricots, peaches, plums, strawberries, raspberries, melon (Warning: offer tiny amounts of soft berry fruits as some children may be allergic to them.)
- chicken
- mild-tasting fresh or frozen fish – plaice, cod, haddock, trout
- small quantities of very lean red meat
- small quantities of split peas and red lentils, and very well-cooked or canned whole chickpeas and beans
- gluten-free cereals – rice, cornflour (cornstarch)

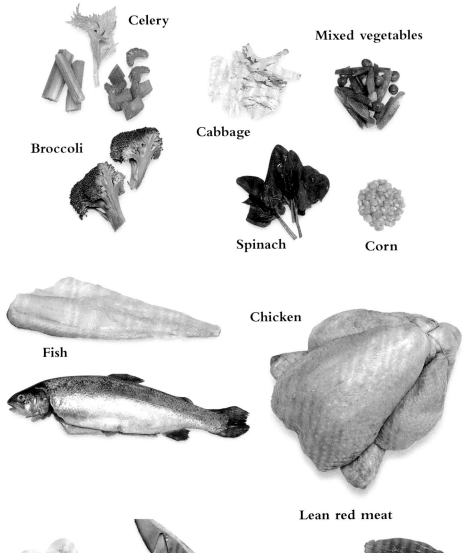

Celery

Mixed vegetables

Cabbage

Broccoli

Spinach

Corn

Fish

Chicken

Lean red meat

Plums

Apricots

Banana

Melon

Above: *Every day brings a new taste: these young gourmets can't wait!*

FOODS TO AVOID
- gluten-based cereals, wheat flour and bread
- cow's milk and milk products
- eggs
- citrus and berry fruits
- nuts, ground or whole
- honey
- fatty foods
- salt and highly spiced foods

Below: *Even healthy adult foods such as wholewheat bread and oranges should be avoided.*

Chickpeas

Cocoa

Split peas

Cornflour (cornstarch)

Lentils

Rice

Autumn Harvest

Makes: 600ml/1 pint/2½ cups

115g/4oz carrot

115g/4oz parsnip

115g/4oz swede (rutabaga)

115g/4oz potato

300ml/½ pint/1¼ cups formula milk

1 Trim and peel the carrot, parsnip, swede and potato, and place in a colander. Rinse under cold water, drain and chop.

2 Place the chopped vegetables in a pan with the formula milk, then bring to the boil, cover and simmer for 20 minutes, or until they are very soft.

3 Purée, mash or sieve (strain) the vegetables until they are smooth.

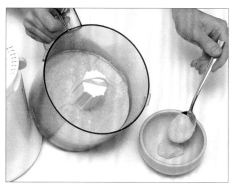

4 Spoon a little into a bowl. Test the temperature and cool if necessary, before giving to the baby.

5 Cover the remaining food and transfer to the refrigerator as soon as possible. Use within 24 hours.

• Suitable for freezing.

TIP
Thin the purée down with a little extra formula milk if your baby prefers a very soft purée.

Mixed Vegetable Platter

Makes: 600ml/1 pint/2½ cups

115g/4oz carrot

175g/6oz potato

115g/4oz broccoli

50g/2oz green cabbage

300ml/½ pint/1¼ cups formula milk

1 Peel the carrot and potato. Rinse, chop and place in a pan. Wash the broccoli and cabbage and cut the broccoli into florets and the stems into thin slices. Shred the cabbage finely.

2 Add the milk to the carrot and potato, bring to the boil, then cover and simmer for 10 minutes.

3 Add the broccoli stems and florets and cabbage, and cook, covered, for 10 minutes, until all the vegetables are tender.

4 Purée, mash or sieve (strain) the vegetables until smooth.

5 Spoon a little into a bowl. Test the temperature and cool if necessary, before giving to the baby.

6 Cover the remaining food and transfer to the refrigerator as soon as possible. Use within 24 hours.

• Suitable for freezing.

Carrot, Lentil and Coriander Purée

Makes: 600ml/1 pint/2½ cups

350g/12oz carrots

175g/6oz potato

50g/2oz/¼ cup red lentils

2.5ml/½ tsp ground coriander

300ml/½ pint/1¼ cups formula milk

1 Trim and peel the carrots and potatoes and then chop into small cubes and place in a pan. Rinse the lentils thoroughly, discarding any black bits.

2 Add the lentils, coriander and milk to the pan and bring to the boil, then cover and simmer for 40 minutes, until the lentils are very soft. Top up with a little extra boiling water if necessary.

TIP

The mixture thickens on cooling so any remaining mixture will need to be thinned slightly with a little formula milk before reheating for the next meal.

3 Purée, mash or sieve (strain) the mixture until smooth.

4 Spoon a little into a bowl. Test the temperature and cool if necessary, before giving to the baby.

5 Cover the remaining purée and transfer to the refrigerator as soon as possible. Use within 24 hours.

• Suitable for freezing.

Red Pepper Risotto

Makes: 600ml/1 pint/2½ cups

50g/2oz/¼ cup long grain rice

300ml/½ pint/1¼ cups formula milk

75g/3oz red (bell) pepper

75g/3oz courgette (zucchini)

50g/2oz celery

1 Place the rice and milk in a pan, bring to the boil and simmer, uncovered, for 5 minutes.

2 Discard the core and seeds from the pepper and trim the courgette and celery. Place the vegetables in a colander and rinse under cold water, then chop them into small pieces.

3 Add the vegetables to the rice mixture, bring to the boil, cover and simmer for about 10 minutes, or until the rice is soft.

• Suitable for freezing.

4 Purée, mash or sieve (strain) the rice mixture until smooth.

5 Spoon a little into a bowl. Test the temperature and cool if necessary, before giving to the baby.

6 Cover the remaining food and transfer to the refrigerator as soon as possible. Use within 24 hours.

Parsnip and Broccoli Mix

Makes: 600ml/1 pint/2½ cups

225g/8oz parsnips

115g/4oz broccoli

300ml/½ pint/1¼ cups formula milk

1 Trim and peel the parsnips and place in a colander with the broccoli. Rinse the parsnips and broccoli under cold water. Chop the parsnips and cut the broccoli into florets, slicing the stems.

2 Put the parsnips in a pan with the milk, bring to the boil, then cover and simmer for about 10 minutes.

3 Add the broccoli and simmer for a further 10 minutes, until the vegetables are soft.

4 Purée, mash or sieve (strain) the vegetable mixture to make a completely smooth purée.

5 Spoon a little into a bowl. Test the temperature and cool if necessary, before giving to the baby.

6 Cover the remaining purée and transfer to the refrigerator as soon as possible. Use within 24 hours.

• Suitable for freezing.

Turkey Stew with Carrots and Corn

Makes: 600ml/1 pint/2½ cups

175g/6oz potato

175g/6oz carrot

115g/4oz turkey breast, skinned and boned

50g/2oz/⅓ cup frozen corn

300ml/½ pint/1¼ cups formula milk

1 Trim and peel the potato and carrots, rinse under cold water and then chop into small cubes.

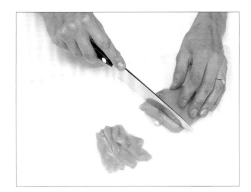

2 Rinse the turkey and cut into thin strips. Place in a small pan with the potato and carrot.

TIP

Bring the mixture to the boil in a flameproof casserole and transfer to a preheated oven 180°C/350°F/Gas 4 and cook for 1¼ hours if preferred.

3 Add the corn and milk. Cover and simmer for 20 minutes, until the turkey is cooked. Purée, mash or sieve (strain) the mixture until smooth.

4 Spoon a little into a bowl. Test the temperature and cool if necessary, before giving to the baby.

5 Cover the remaining food and refrigerate. Use within 24 hours.

• Suitable for freezing.

Chicken and Parsnip Purée

Makes: 600ml/1 pint/2½ cups

350g/12oz parsnips

115g/4oz chicken breast, skinned
   and boned

300ml/½ pint/1¼ cups formula milk

1 Peel the parsnips, and trim the woody tops and bottoms. Rinse and chop roughly.

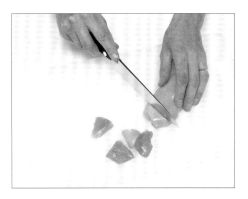

2 Rinse the chicken under cold water and cut into small pieces.

3 Place the parsnips, chicken and milk in a pan. Cover and simmer for 20 minutes, or until the parsnips are tender.

4 Purée, mash or sieve (strain) the mixture until smooth.

5 Spoon into a bowl. Test the temperature and cool if necessary, before giving to the baby.

6 Cover the remaining purée and transfer to the refrigerator as soon as possible. Use within 24 hours.

• Suitable for freezing.

TIP

For a very smooth purée, drain all the liquid into a liquidizer and add half the solids, blend until smooth, then add the remaining ingredients. If using a food processor, add all the solids and a little liquid, process until smooth, then add the remaining liquid.

Cock-a-Leekie Casserole

Makes: 600ml/1 pint/2½ cups

50g/2oz leek

275g/10oz potatoes

115g/4oz chicken breast, skinned and boned

300ml/½ pint/1¼ cups formula milk

1 Halve the leek lengthways and rinse under running water to remove any dirt or grit.

2 Peel potatoes and cut into small dice. Rinse the chicken and cut into pieces and thinly slice the leek.

3 Place the vegetables and chicken in a pan with the milk.

4 Bring the mixture to the boil, cover with a lid and simmer gently for 20 minutes, until the potatoes are just tender. Purée, mash or sieve (strain) the mixture until it is completely smooth.

TIP
You can vary the texture of this recipe depending on how you purée the mixture. A fine sieve (strainer) produces the finest consistency, then a food processor, while a food mill gives the coarsest texture. Starchy vegetables thicken the purée and bind it together. Any root vegetable can be used for this recipe, but make sure it is thoroughly cooked before blending.

5 Spoon a little into a bowl. Test the temperature and cool if necessary, before giving to the baby. Use within 24 hours.

• Suitable for freezing.

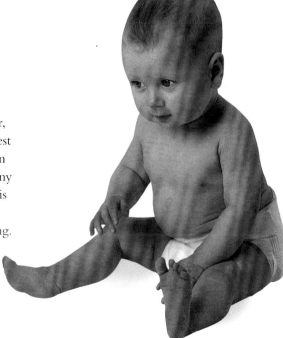

Trout and Courgette Savoury

Makes: 600ml/1 pint/2½ cups

275g/10oz potatoes

175g/6oz courgettes (zucchini)

115g/4oz pink trout fillet

250ml/8fl oz/1 cup formula milk

1 Peel the potatoes, trim the courgettes and rinse under cold water. Dice the potatoes and cut the courgettes into slices.

2 Place the vegetables in a pan. Rinse the trout and arrange on top, then pour over the milk. Bring to the boil, cover and simmer for 15 minutes, until the potatoes and fish are cooked.

3 Lift the trout out of the pan and peel off the skin. Break it into pieces with a knife and fork, checking carefully for any bones.

4 Purée, mash or sieve (strain) the fish, the vegetables and the liquid until quite smooth.

5 Spoon a little into a bowl. Test the temperature and cool if necessary, before giving to the baby.

6 Cover any remaining food and transfer to the refrigerator as soon as possible. Use within 24 hours.

• Suitable for freezing.

Fisherman's Pie

Makes: 600ml/1 pint/2½ cups

350g/12oz potatoes

90g/3½oz brick frozen skinless cod

25g/1oz/¼ cup frozen peas

25g/1oz/2 tbsp frozen corn

300ml/½ pint/1¼ cups formula milk

1 Peel and rinse the potatoes and cut into even pieces. Place in a pan with the fish, peas, corn and milk.

2 Bring to the boil, cover and simmer for 15 minutes, until the potatoes are very tender.

3 Lift the fish out of the pan and break into pieces with a knife and fork, checking carefully and removing any small bones.

5 Spoon a little into a bowl. Test the temperature and cool if necessary, before giving to the baby.

6 Cover the remaining purée and place in the refrigerator as soon as possible. Use within 24 hours.

● Suitable for freezing.

4 Purée, mash or sieve (strain) the fish, vegetables and cooking liquid until completely smooth.

Apple Ambrosia

Makes: 300ml/½ pint/1¼ cups

1 eating apple

25g/1oz flaked rice

300ml/½ pint/1¼ cups formula milk

1 Quarter, core and peel the apple. Slice thinly and place in a pan with the rice and milk.

2 Bring to the boil then simmer over a gentle heat for 10–12 minutes, until the rice is soft, stirring occasionally with a wooden spoon.

3 Purée or mash the apple and rice mixture until completely smooth.

4 Spoon into a bowl. Test the temperature and cool if necessary, before giving to the baby. Cover the remaining purée and transfer to the refrigerator as soon as possible. Use within 24 hours.

VARIATION
Chocolate Pudding
Cook the rice as above but without the apple. Stir 25g/1oz milk chocolate dots and 15ml/1 tbsp caster (superfine) sugar into the hot rice and then purée or mash until smooth. Spoon into small dishes and cool as necessary.

Fruit Salad Purée

Makes: 350ml/12fl oz/1½ cups

1 nectarine or peach

1 dessert apple

1 ripe pear

25g/1oz fresh or frozen raspberries
  or strawberries

1 Halve the nectarine or peach, discard the stone (pit), then peel and chop. Peel, quarter and core the apple and pear and slice thinly.

2 Put the prepared fruits, the hulled raspberries or strawberries and 15ml/1 tbsp water in a pan. Cover and simmer for 10 minutes, until the fruit is soft.

3 Press the mixture through a sieve (strainer) or process and then sieve (strain) to remove the berry pips (seeds). Discard the pips.

4 Spoon a little into a baby bowl. Test the temperature and cool if necessary, before giving to the baby.

5 Cover the remaining purée and transfer to the refrigerator as soon as possible. Use within 24 hours.

● Suitable for freezing.

TIP
Babies tend to eat smaller quantities of dessert, so it is best to open freeze purée in a sterilized ice cube tray. Transfer the cubes to a plastic bag once frozen.

VARIATION
Peach and Melon Blush
To make 175ml/6fl oz/¾ cup, take 1 ripe peach and ¼ ripe Charentais melon. Peel and halve the peach, discard the stone (pit) and cut up the fruit. Scoop the seeds out of the melon and cut away the skin. Roughly chop the melon into pieces.
  Purée or sieve (strain) the fruit until completely smooth. Spoon a little into a bowl and serve.

STAGE 3: SEVEN TO NINE MONTHS

FROM SEVEN TO NINE MONTHS IS A RAPID DEVELOPMENT PERIOD FOR YOUR BABY. BY EIGHT MONTHS, BABIES ARE USUALLY QUITE GOOD AT HOLDING THINGS, SO LET YOUR BABY HOLD A SECOND SPOON WHILE YOU ARE FEEDING HER, TO HELP DEVELOP CO-ORDINATION. THIS IS THE FIRST STEP TOWARDS SELF-FEEDING. ALL THE RECIPES FROM THE PREVIOUS SECTION CAN STILL BE MADE FOR YOUR GROWING BABY; JUST ADJUST THE TEXTURE SO THAT FOODS ARE SLIGHTLY COARSER.

Suitable Foods

FOODS TO INCLUDE

- wheat-based foods, pasta, bread – first fingers (thin slices) of toast or bread sticks
- breakfast cereals such as those made up with cow's milk
- cow's milk and dairy foods, e.g. yogurt, cottage cheese, mild Cheddar and Edam cheese
- red meat, but make sure you trim off fat and gristle
- hard-boiled egg yolk
- citrus fruits
- fingers of cooked carrot, broccoli
- smooth peanut butter

Breakfast cereal

Breakfast cereal

Mild cheeses

Yogurt

Lean red meat

Cottage cheese

Pasta

Bread

Cooked egg yolk

Citrus fruit

Peanut butter

Fish

Broccoli and carrot

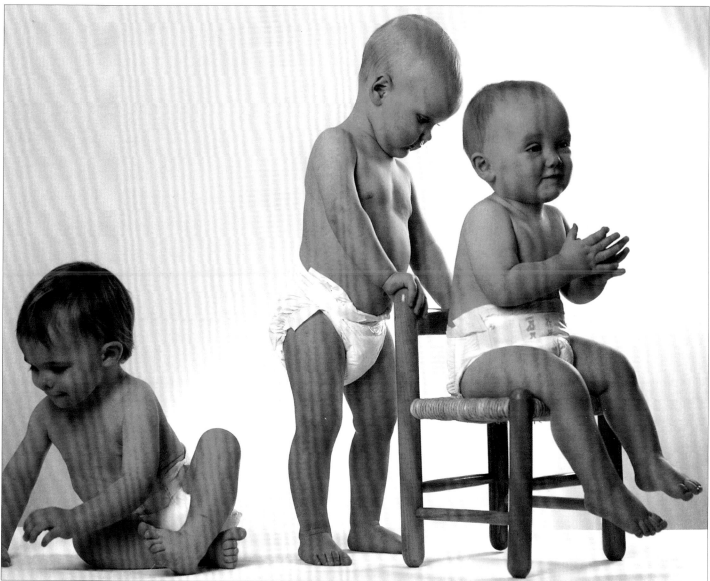

Above: *From seven to nine months your baby will develop rapidly.*

FOODS TO AVOID

- egg white
- whole or chopped nuts
- canned fish in brine
- organ meats – liver, kidney
- chillies and other very spicy foods
- salty foods
- sugary foods

Right: *There is still a wide range of fatty, salty and spicy foods that must be avoided.*

Shepherd's Pie

Makes: 600ml/1 pint/2¹/₂ cups

2 tomatoes

¹/₄ onion

225g/8oz potato

50g/2oz button (white) mushrooms

115g/4oz lean minced (ground) beef

250ml/8fl oz/1 cup water

15ml/1 tbsp tomato ketchup

pinch of dried mixed herbs

4 Add the tomatoes, potato, mushrooms and onion and cook for a further 3 minutes. Stir well to blend all the flavours together.

5 Add the water, ketchup and herbs. Bring to the boil, then reduce the heat, cover and simmer for 40 minutes, until the meat and vegetables are tender.

6 Process or mash the meat and vegetables just enough to give the desired consistency.

7 Spoon a little into a bowl. Test the temperature and cool if necessary, before giving to the baby.

8 Cover the remainder and refrigerate. Use within 24 hours.

1 Make a cross cut in each tomato, put in a small bowl and cover with boiling water. Leave to stand for 1 minute and then drain and peel off the skins. Cut into quarters and scoop out the seeds.

2 Finely chop the onion, chop the potato and slice the mushrooms.

3 Dry-fry the beef in a pan for 5 minutes, stirring until browned all over.

• Suitable for freezing.

Braised Beef and Carrots

Makes: 600ml/1 pint/2½ cups

175g/6oz potato

225g/8oz carrots

¼ onion

175g/6oz stewing beef

300ml/½ pint/1¼ cups water

pinch of dried mixed herbs

1 Preheat the oven to 180°C/ 350°F/Gas 4. Peel and chop the potato, carrots and onion, and place in a flameproof casserole.

2 Rinse the beef, cut away any fat and gristle and cut into small cubes using a sharp knife.

3 Add the meat, water and herbs to the casserole, bring to the boil and then cover and cook in the oven for 1½ hours, or until the meat is tender and the vegetables are soft.

4 Process or mash the ingredients to the desired consistency and spoon a little into a bowl. Test the temperature and cool if necessary, before giving to the baby.

5 Cover any unused food and transfer to the refrigerator as soon as possible. Use within 24 hours.

• Suitable for freezing.

TIP
Replace the carrots with any other root vegetable, such as parsnip or swede (rutabaga), if wished.

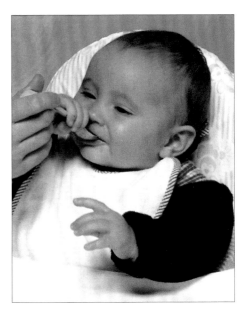

Lamb Hotpot

Makes: 600ml/1 pint/2½ cups

| 115g/4oz potato |
| 115g/4oz carrot |
| 115g/4oz swede (rutabaga) |
| 50g/2oz leek |
| 115g/4oz lamb fillet |
| 300ml/½ pint/1¼ cup water |
| pinch of dried rosemary |

1 Peel the potato, carrot and swede, then rinse and chop into small cubes. Halve the leek lengthways, rinse well and slice. Place all the vegetables in a pan.

2 Rinse the lamb under cold water and chop into small pieces, discarding any fat.

3 Add the meat to the pan with the water and rosemary. Bring to the boil, cover and simmer for 30 minutes or until the lamb is thoroughly cooked.

4 Process or mash the ingredients to the desired consistency.

5 Spoon a little into a bowl, test the temperature and cool if necessary, before giving to the baby.

6 Cover the remaining food and transfer to the refrigerator as soon as possible. Use within 24 hours.

• Suitable for freezing.

Lamb and Lentil Savoury

Makes: 600ml/1 pint/2½ cups

115g/4oz lamb fillet

115g/4oz swede (rutabaga)

1 celery stick

25g/1oz/2 tbsp red lentils

15ml/1 tbsp tomato ketchup

350ml/12fl oz/1½ cups water

1 Rinse the lamb under cold water, trim off any fat and chop into small pieces. Peel the swede, place in a colander with the celery and rinse with cold water. Chop into cubes and place in a pan.

2 Put the lentils in a sieve (strainer) and rinse under cold water, picking out any black bits. Add to the pan with the lamb and ketchup.

3 Add the water and bring to the boil, then cover and simmer for 40 minutes, or until the lentils are soft. Top up with extra water during cooking if necessary, then process or mash just enough to give the desired consistency.

4 Spoon a little into a bowl, test the temperature and cool if necessary, before giving to the baby.

5 Cover the remaining food and transfer to the refrigerator as soon as possible. Use within 24 hours.

● Suitable for freezing.

VARIATION
Substitute green lentils or split peas for the red lentils and a small courgette (zucchini) for the celery stick.

Country Pork and Runner Beans

Makes: 450ml/¾ pint/1⅞ cups

115g/4oz lean pork

115g/4oz potato

115g/4oz carrot

75g/3oz runner (green) beans

pinch of dried sage

350ml/12fl oz/1½ cups water

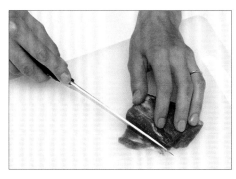

1 Rinse the pork under cold water, trim away any fat and gristle and chop into small cubes.

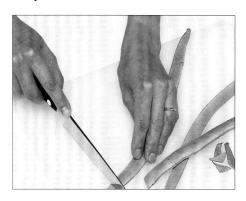

2 Peel the potato and carrot, trim the beans, rinse and chop.

TIPS
If runner beans are unavailable use French (green) beans, sugar snap peas or broccoli. Look out for ready-prepared diced pork in the supermarket. Cut into smaller pieces and be sure to remove any gristle before cooking.

3 Put the pork, potato and carrot in a pan with the sage and water. Bring to the boil, cover and simmer for 30 minutes.

4 Add the beans and cook, covered, for a further 10 minutes, until all the vegetables are tender.

5 Process or mash to the desired consistency, then spoon a little into a bowl. Test the temperature before giving to the baby.

6 Cover and transfer the remaining food to the refrigerator. Use within 24 hours.

• Suitable for freezing.

VARIATION
Instead of the pork, use any lean meat in this recipe, such as chicken or turkey. Add broad (fava) beans, with the outer skin removed, in place of the runner beans.

Pork and Apple Savoury

Makes: 600ml/1 pint/2½ cups

175g/6oz lean pork

175g/6oz potato

175g/6oz swede (rutabaga) or parsnip

¼ onion

½ eating apple

300ml/½ pint/1¼ cups water

pinch of dried sage

1 Preheat the oven to 180°C/ 350°F/Gas 4. Rinse the pork under cold water, trim away any fat and gristle, then chop. Peel and chop the vegetables. Peel, core and chop the apple.

2 Put the meat, vegetables, apple, water and sage in a flameproof casserole, cover and bring to the boil, stirring once or twice.

3 Cover and cook in the oven for 1¼ hours, until the meat is tender, then process or mash to the desired consistency.

4 Spoon a little into a bowl, test the temperature and cool if necessary, before giving to the baby.

5 Cover the remaining food and transfer to the refrigerator as soon as possible. Use within 24 hours.

• Suitable for freezing.

TIP
The mixture can be cooked in a pan on the stove for 40 minutes, if preferred.

Nursery Kedgeree

Makes: 600ml/1 pint/2½ cups

50g/2oz/¼ cup long grain rice

25g/1oz/2 tbsp frozen peas

350ml/12fl oz/1½ cups formula milk

90g/3¼oz brick frozen skinless cod

2 hard-boiled egg yolks

1 Place the rice, peas, milk and fish in a pan, bring to the boil, cover and simmer for 15 minutes, until the fish is cooked and the rice is soft.

2 Lift the fish out of the pan and break into pieces with a knife and fork, checking for bones.

3 Stir the fish into the rice mixture and add the egg yolks.

TIP
Peas can be quite difficult to mash down. Check before giving to the baby as whole peas are difficult for her to chew.

4 Mash with a fork to the desired consistency. Alternatively blend in a food processor or liquidizer, or press through a sieve (strainer).

5 Spoon a little into a bowl, test the temperature and cool if necessary, before giving to the baby.

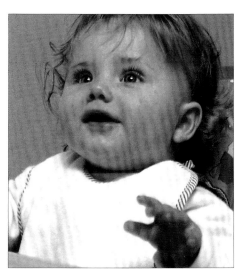

6 Cover the remaining kedgeree and transfer to the refrigerator as soon as possible. Use within 24 hours.

• Suitable for freezing.

Mediterranean Vegetables

Makes: 600ml/1 pint/2½ cups

3 tomatoes

175g/6oz courgettes (zucchini)

75g/3oz button (white) mushrooms

115g/4oz red (bell) pepper

20ml/4 tsp tomato ketchup

250ml/8fl oz/1 cup water

pinch of dried mixed herbs

40g/1½oz dried pasta shapes

1 Make a cross cut in each tomato, put in a small bowl and cover with boiling water. Leave for 1 minute, then drain and peel off the skins. Cut into quarters and scoop out the seeds from the tomatoes.

2 Trim the courgette and mushrooms and cut away the core and seeds from the pepper.

3 Rinse and slice the courgette and mushrooms. Chop the pepper.

4 Put the vegetables in a pan with the ketchup, water and herbs. Cover and simmer for 10 minutes, or until tender.

5 Meanwhile cook the pasta in boiling water for 8–10 minutes, until tender. Drain.

6 Mix the vegetables and pasta together and process or mash.

7 Spoon a little into a bowl, test the temperature and cool if necessary, before giving to the baby.

8 Cover remaining mixture and refrigerate. Use within 24 hours.

• Suitable for freezing.

TIP

For adventurous eaters add ½ clove crushed garlic at Step 3.

Pasta with Sauce

Makes: 600ml/1 pint/2½ cups

115g/4oz carrot

50g/2oz Brussels sprouts

25g/1oz green beans

25g/1oz/2 tbsp frozen corn

50g/2oz dried pasta shapes

350ml/12fl oz/1½ cups formula milk

50g/2oz Cheddar or mild cheese

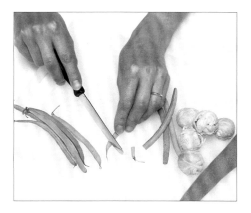

1 Peel the carrot, discard any discoloured outer leaves from the sprouts and trim the beans. Rinse and then chop into pieces.

2 Place the prepared vegetables, corn, pasta and milk in a pan, bring to the boil and then simmer, uncovered, for 12-15 minutes, until the pasta is cooked.

TIP

Vary the vegetables depending on what you have in the refrigerator.

3 Grate the cheese and add to the vegetables, stirring until the cheese has completely melted.

4 Process or mash just enough to give the desired consistency, then spoon a little into a bowl. Test the temperature and cool if necessary, before giving to the baby.

5 Cover the remaining food and transfer to the refrigerator as soon as possible. Use within 24 hours.

• Suitable for freezing.

Apple and Orange Fool

Makes: 250ml/8fl oz/1 cup

2 eating apples

5ml/1 tsp grated orange rind and
 15ml/1 tbsp orange juice

15ml/1 tbsp custard powder

5ml/1 tsp caster (superfine) sugar

150ml/¼ pint/⅔ cup formula milk

1 Quarter, core and peel the apples. Slice and place the apples in a pan with the orange rind and juice.

2 Cover and cook gently for 10 minutes, stirring occasionally until the apples are soft.

3 Blend the custard powder and sugar with a little of the milk to make a smooth paste. Bring the remaining milk to the boil and stir into the custard mixture.

4 Return the custard to the pan and slowly bring to the boil, stirring until thickened and smooth.

5 Process or mash the apple to the desired consistency. Add the custard and stir to mix.

6 Spoon a little into a bowl, test the temperature and cool if necessary, before giving to the baby.

7 Cover the remaining fool and transfer to the refrigerator as soon as possible. Use within 24 hours.

• Suitable for freezing.

Orchard Fruit Dessert

Makes: 450ml/¾ pint/1⅞ cups

1 ripe pear

225g/8oz ripe plums

15ml/1 tbsp caster (superfine) sugar

15ml/1 tbsp custard powder

150ml/¼ pint/⅔ cup formula milk

1 Quarter, core, peel and slice the pear. Wash the plums, then cut in half, stone (pit) and slice.

2 Put the fruit in a pan with 15ml/1 tbsp water and 10ml/2 tsp of the sugar. Cover and cook gently for 10 minutes, until soft.

3 Blend the custard powder, remaining sugar and a little of the milk to make a smooth paste.

4 Bring the remaining milk to the boil and gradually stir into the custard mixture. Pour the custard back into the pan and bring to the boil, stirring, until it is both thickened and smooth.

5 Process or mash the fruit to the desired consistency and stir in the custard. Spoon a little into a bowl, test the temperature and cool if necessary, before giving to the baby.

6 Cover the remaining custard and transfer to the refrigerator as soon as possible. Use within 24 hours.

- Suitable for freezing.

Peach Melba Dessert

Makes: 175ml/6fl oz/³⁄₄ cup

1 ripe peach

25g/1oz fresh or frozen raspberries

15ml/1 tbsp icing (confectioners') sugar

115g/4oz Greek (US strained plain) yogurt

1 Halve the peach, discard the stone (pit), then peel and slice. Place in a pan with the raspberries and 15ml/1 tbsp water.

2 Cover and cook gently for 10 minutes, until soft.

3 Purée and press through a sieve (strainer) to remove the raspberry pips (seeds).

TIP
The finished dessert is not suitable for freezing, but the sweetened fruit purée can be frozen in sections of an ice-cube tray. Defrost cubes of purée and mix each cube with 15ml/1 tbsp yogurt.

4 Set aside to cool, then stir in the sugar and swirl in the yogurt. Spoon a little into a baby dish.

5 Cover the remaining dessert and transfer to the refrigerator. Use within 24 hours.

VARIATION
Bananarama
To make a single portion, use ½ a small banana and 15ml/1 tbsp of Greek (US strained plain) yogurt. Mash the banana until smooth and add the yogurt. Stir to mix and serve immediately. Do not make this dessert in advance, as the banana will discolour while standing.

STAGE 4: NINE TO TWELVE MONTHS

G RADUALLY PROGRESS FROM MINCED (GROUND) TO CHOPPED OR ROUGHLY MASHED FOOD. BY NOW YOUR BABY WILL BE ABLE TO JOIN IN WITH FAMILY MEALS AND EAT A LITTLE OF WHAT YOU ARE EATING. ENSURE THAT YOUR BABY IS EATING THREE MAIN MEALS AND TWO TO THREE SNACK MEALS PER DAY. YOUNG CHILDREN DEVELOP AT AN INCREDIBLY FAST RATE AND SO NEED TO EAT LITTLE AND OFTEN TO SUSTAIN ENERGY AND GROWTH LEVELS. AGAIN, FOODS FROM THE PREVIOUS SECTIONS CAN STILL BE SERVED TO YOUR BABY; JUST ADJUST THE TEXTURES AS NECESSARY.

Suitable Foods

FOODS TO INCLUDE
- whole eggs
- finely ground nuts
- more flavourings – stock (bouillon) cubes if part of a family-size casserole
- greater selection of finger foods – slices of peeled fruit (such as dessert apple or pear), raw carrot and cucumber sticks, small squares of cooked chicken

- selection of foods from the four main food groups – carbohydrates (cereals, bread, potatoes, rice, pasta); fruit and vegetables; protein (meat, poultry, fish, eggs, beans, peas, lentils, tofu, nuts); milk and milk products (cheese, yogurt, butter).

Apple, carrot and cucumber

Ground nuts

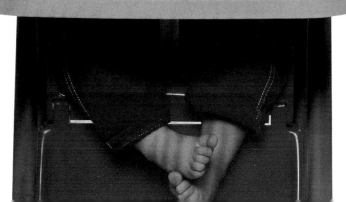

Whole egg

Left: *Finger foods – such as chopped raw vegetables and fruit pieces – come into their own at this age, and children love to help themselves.*

Above and below right: *Active children develop at a fast rate and need to eat little and often to sustain their energy levels.*

Below: *Though now a very small list, there are still some foods it is important to omit.*

FOODS TO AVOID
- keep salt to a minimum and omit if possible
- sugar: add just enough to make the food appetizing without being overly sweet
- honey

- fat: trim visible fat off raw meat, grill rather than fry
- organ meats – liver, kidney

I can feed myself!

Encouraging your baby to feed herself can be a truly messy business. Some babies are interested from a very early age, and those little fingers seem to move like lightning grabbing the bowl or the spoon you're using to feed them with. Give your baby a second spoon to play with, leaving you more able to spoon in the lunch.

As your baby grows, offer her a few finger foods to hold and hopefully eat, while you continue to feed from a spoon. Cooked carrot sticks, broccoli and cauliflower florets are soft on a young mouth and easy to chew. As your baby grows, you can introduce bread sticks and toast fingers.

Encourage your baby to pick up foods, and as her co-ordination improves and she gets the idea, more food will actually go where it is intended. Try to cut down on the mess by rolling up your baby's sleeves and covering clothes with a large bib, preferably with sleeves.

Above: *A bib with sleeves.*

Remove any hair bands and have a wet flannel at the ready.

Although it is tempting not to allow a baby to feed herself, try not to be frustrated by the mess. Babies that are encouraged to feed themselves will probably be more adventurous later on, and you will probably find there is less mess than with a baby who is always spoon fed

TEACHING YOUR BABY TO FEED HIMSELF

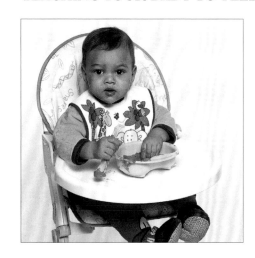

1 Cover your baby well – this can be very messy! Give him a spoon of his own to play with.

2 While you are feeding your baby, allow him to play with the food – with his hands or the spoon.

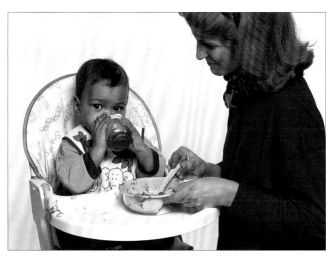

3 Let your baby use the cup and spoon by himself. Don't worry about spillage – there are bound to be lots of slips at this stage.

4 Keep tissues or a damp flannel available and clean as you go. Be patient and take things slowly.

Above and below right: *Active children develop at a fast rate and need to eat little and often to sustain their energy levels.*

Below: *Though now a very small list, there are still some foods it is important to omit.*

FOODS TO AVOID
- keep salt to a minimum and omit if possible
- sugar: add just enough to make the food appetizing without being overly sweet
- honey
- fat: trim visible fat off raw meat, grill rather than fry
- organ meats – liver, kidney

I can feed myself!

Encouraging your baby to feed herself can be a truly messy business. Some babies are interested from a very early age, and those little fingers seem to move like lightning grabbing the bowl or the spoon you're using to feed them with. Give your baby a second spoon to play with, leaving you more able to spoon in the lunch.

As your baby grows, offer her a few finger foods to hold and hopefully eat, while you continue to feed from a spoon. Cooked carrot sticks, broccoli and cauliflower florets are soft on a young mouth and easy to chew. As your baby grows, you can introduce bread sticks and toast fingers.

Encourage your baby to pick up foods, and as her co-ordination improves and she gets the idea, more food will actually go where it is intended. Try to cut down on the mess by rolling up your baby's sleeves and covering clothes with a large bib, preferably with sleeves.

Above: *A bib with sleeves.*

Remove any hair bands and have a wet flannel at the ready.

Although it is tempting not to allow a baby to feed herself, try not to be frustrated by the mess. Babies that are encouraged to feed themselves will probably be more adventurous later on, and you will probably find there is less mess than with a baby who is always spoon fed

TEACHING YOUR BABY TO FEED HIMSELF

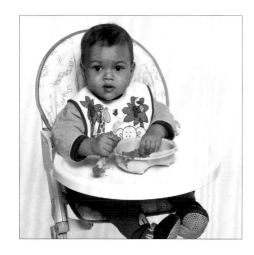

1 Cover your baby well – this can be very messy! Give him a spoon of his own to play with.

2 While you are feeding your baby, allow him to play with the food – with his hands or the spoon.

3 Let your baby use the cup and spoon by himself. Don't worry about spillage – there are bound to be lots of slips at this stage.

4 Keep tissues or a damp flannel available and clean as you go. Be patient and take things slowly.

and keeps grabbing at the bowl. In addition, she will be able to join in your family meals and also give you the chance to eat your own meal before it gets cold.

WHAT TO DO IF YOUR CHILD CHOKES
● Don't waste time trying to remove food from your baby's mouth unless it can be done easily.
● Turn your baby, head down, supporting her head with your forearm and slap firmly between the shoulder blades.
● If this does not work, try again.
● Don't hesitate to ring your doctor or emergency services if worried.

Above: *Don't be afraid to take quick, firm action in an emergency.*

COPING WITH THE MESS
As babies grow so too does the amount of mess! It is incredible how just a few tablespoons of lunch can be spread across so many surfaces and so many items of clothing.
● Choose a large bib. Fabric bibs with a plastic liner are the most comfortable for babies to wear when tiny, moving on to a plastic pelican-style bib to catch food as they grow older. Check the back of your baby's neck as these can rub.

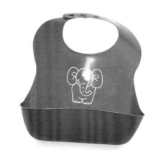

Above: *A hard plastic "pelican" bib.*

● If you plan to feed your baby in the dining room, then protect the carpet with an old sheet, pieces of newspaper, or a plastic tablecloth or groundsheet. It is vital to take this with you if visiting friends.
● Give your baby a second spoon or small toy to play with so that she doesn't try to grab the laden spoon that you are holding.

Left: *It is a real delight when your baby can begin to eat independently. Not only can you start to eat with your baby, and relax a little more, but he will also enjoy setting his own pace and eating his meal in the order he chooses. At this stage, the family can usually return to eating together around the table as a group.*

Above: *A plastic tablecloth or groundsheet on the floor will prevent carpet stains.*

FINGER FOODS

Finger foods are not only fun to eat but help your baby's co-ordination. Snacks play an important part in a young child's diet as appetites may be small, but energy and growth needs are great. Choose foods that are nutrient dense and avoid sweet sugary snacks such as chocolate biscuits (cookies).

Above: *Your baby can eat at his own pace until he is full.*

Plums

Grapes

Celery

Carrots

Mini-sandwiches

Chicken pieces

Fish fingers (breaded fish sticks

Toast triangles

Cheese cubes

Ham

Marmite fingers

TIPS

- Make sure the baby is comfortable either on your lap or strapped into a baby chair or high-chair.
- Check the temperature of the food and make sure it is not too hot.
- Change the texture of the food: some babies like quite wet mixtures, some hate lumps, some like a few lumps for interest, others prefer food they can pick up – mini ham sandwiches, thick slices of grilled fish fingers (breaded fish sticks), even picking up peas and corn.
- Encourage your baby to feed herself; don't worry about the mess – your baby is still learning – but just mop up at the end.

- Try to keep calm. If your baby keeps spitting food out, you may find it less upsetting to offer bought food rather than home-made so you don't feel you've wasted time cooking.
- Try not to let your baby see you're upset or annoyed. Even a one-year-old can sense the power she can have over you.
- If solid meals are well established, give her a drink at the end of the meal so that she is not full with milk before she begins.
- Avoid biscuits (cookies) and sweet things – your baby will soon learn that if she makes a fuss when the savoury is offered, dessert will soon follow.

- Remember no baby will starve herself. Often babies who have been good eaters become more difficult to feed. Continue offering a variety of food and don't despair.

Above: *Give drinks at the end of the meal, or they will fill your baby up before he eats.*

Coping with a fussy eater

All children are fussy eaters at some stage. If meal-times are always calm and plates always clean, then your family must be one in a million. Even very young children learn the power they have over their parents, and meal-times give them a great opportunity to exercise it.

THE BABY SEEMS TO HAVE A SMALL APPETITE

Babies' appetites, like adults', vary enormously. Don't force feed your baby; if she's been eating well and then turns her head away or starts spitting out the food, it's a clear indication that she's had enough, even if the amount seems very small to you. Resist the temptation to encourage your baby to clear the dish: it is never helpful to force children of any age, and can be extremely counter-productive. Towards the end of the first year, a baby's weight gain usually slows down, and babies who have been good eaters become more difficult to feed. If you're worried, talk to your health visitor or doctor and regularly check your baby's weight.

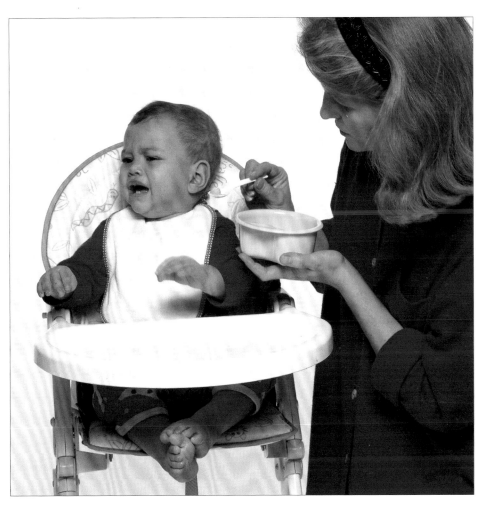

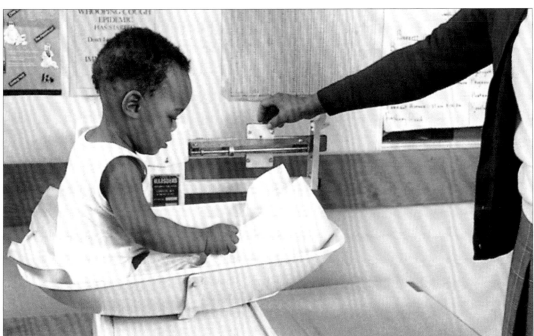

Above: *Don't worry when you encounter resistance in feeding: there never has been a baby that likes all foods, all the time.*

Left: *If you have any serious anxieties, see your doctor or health visitor and get your baby's weight checked regularly.*

The Importance of a Varied Diet

Once your baby progresses to more varied fruit and vegetable purées you are really beginning to lay down the foundations for a healthy eating pattern and sound nutritional habits that will take your baby through childhood and into adult life.

It is vitally important to include portions of food from each of the four main food groups – carbohydrates such as cereal, pasta and bread; fruit and vegetables; protein such as meat, fish and eggs; milk and milk products – every day. Don't forget to make sure that the types of food you choose are suitable for the age of your child.

Left: *Your baby is now at the age where the diet can and should be as diverse as any adult's. Variety is crucial for health reasons, and also has the benefit of allowing you many options for encouraging and maintaining the kind of interest in all types of food that will ensure good eating habits develop for the future.*

Group 1: *Cereals, bread, potatoes, rice and pasta.*

Group 2: *Fruit and vegetables* – bland tastes to start, such as potato, swede (rutabaga) and parsnip, then stronger flavours and a wider variety.

Group 3: *Meat and meat alternatives* – meat, poultry, fish, eggs, peas, beans, lentils, tofu, finely ground nuts.

Group 4: *Milk and milk products* – milk, including soya milk, cheese, yogurt (plain at first, then flavoured).

Group 5: *Sugars*

Group 6: *Fats and oils*

There are two more food groups that add palatability to the diet as well as contributing energy.

It is not recommended that you add sugar to baby foods or give lots of sugary drinks, particularly in the early days of weaning. Many of us have an inherent need for sweetness, but to cater to this without building in bad habits, try and include foods in the diet that are naturally sweet. Choose dessert apples instead of very sharp cooking apples, and mix bananas or ripe apricots with sharper-tasting fruits.

For those foods that are very sharp try to add 5ml/1tsp sugar per portion, so they become palatable without being overly sweet. Given the choice, your baby would prefer sweet flavours to savoury, so make sure you include a good range of tastes in the diet. Too much sugar or too many sweetened foods or drinks at this stage could lead to tooth decay

before the teeth are even through. Try to avoid offering biscuits (cookies) as a mid-morning or afternoon snack. Instead, encourage your baby to eat:
- a piece of banana
- a plain bread roll
- a few triangles of toast
- a milky drink
- a small container of yogurt

Watch the amounts of fat and oil you include in the diet. Avoid frying, especially when preparing first foods, as young babies have difficulty digesting such foods. As your baby develops, you can spread toast fingers with a little butter or margarine as easy-to-hold finger food. Maintain the milk feeds and introduce full-fat (whole) cow's milk after one year as the main drink of the day. Don't be tempted to serve skimmed (skim) milk, as the valuable fat-soluble vitamins A and D will be lost, and your baby may not get the energy needed for growth.

HOME-MADE OR MANUFACTURED FOODS?

Most parents use a combination of the two. Bought baby foods are convenient and often easier to use if going out for the day or until your baby's meals coincide with those of the rest of the family. Dried baby foods can be useful

Above: *A piece of fruit or chopped vegetable is always preferable to a biscuit.*

in the very early days, when your baby is eating only a teaspoon of food at each meal. On the other hand, home-made foods can be batch-cooked or made with some of the ingredients from the main family meal and are often less trouble than you might expect. Added to this is the satisfaction of knowing your baby has eaten a wholesome meal and hopefully is acquiring a taste for home cooking.

Left: *Home-made foods have the advantage that you know exactly what is in them. But there are some excellent products available for purchase that can save you time and effort and add hugely to your repertoire without any loss of dietary value.*

Lamb Couscous

Makes: 750ml/1¼ pint/3 cups

115g/4oz carrot

115g/4oz swede (rutabaga)

¼ onion

175g/6oz lamb fillet

5ml/1 tsp oil

10ml/2 tsp vegetable purée (paste)

30ml/2 tbsp currants or raisins

300ml/½ pint/1¼ cups water

50g/2oz couscous

1 Peel the carrot, swede and onion, rinse and chop. Rinse the lamb, trim off any fat, and chop.

2 Heat the oil in a pan, and fry the lamb until browned.

3 Add the vegetables, cook for 2 minutes, then stir in the vegetable purée, currants and water. Cover and simmer for 25 minutes.

4 Put the couscous in a sieve (strainer) and rinse under cold running water. Cover and steam the couscous over the lamb pan, for 5 minutes.

5 Chop or process the lamb mixture to the desired consistency. Fluff up the couscous with a fork and add to the lamb mixture stirring well.

6 Spoon a little into a bowl, test the temperature and cool if necessary, before giving to the baby.

7 Cover the remaining food and transfer to the refrigerator as soon as possible. Use within 24 hours.

- Suitable for freezing.

TIP
Look out for vegetable purée in tubes on the same shelf as the tomato purée in the supermarket.

Paprika Pork

Makes: 600ml/1 pint/2½ cups

175g/6oz lean pork

75g/3oz carrot

175g/6oz potato

¼ onion

¼ red (bell) pepper

5ml/1tsp oil

2.5ml/½ tsp paprika

150g/5oz/⅔ cup baked beans

150ml/¼ pint/⅔ cup water

1 Preheat the oven to 180°C/ 350°F/Gas 4. Rinse the pork under cold water, pat dry and trim away any fat or gristle. Cut the pork into small cubes.

2 Peel the carrot, potato and onion. Cut away the core and remove any seeds from the pepper. Put into a colander, rinse under cold water, then chop into small pieces.

3 Heat the oil in a flameproof casserole, add the pork and fry for a few minutes, stirring until browned. Add the vegetables, cook for 2 minutes, then add the paprika, baked beans and water.

4 Bring back to the boil, then cover and cook in the oven for 1¼ hours, until the pork is tender.

5 Chop or process the casserole to the desired consistency, then spoon a little into a bowl. Test the temperature and cool if necessary, before giving to the baby.

6 Cover the remaining food and transfer to the refrigerator as soon as possible. Use within 24 hours.

● Suitable for freezing.

TIP

If using a food processor to chop the baby's dinner, drain off most of the liquid. Process, then stir in enough liquid for desired texture.

Chicken and Celery Supper

Makes: 600ml/1 pint/2½ cups

175g/6oz chicken thighs, skinned and boned

¼ onion

225g/8oz carrots

75g/3oz celery

5ml/1 tsp oil

10ml/2 tsp vegetable purée (paste)

250ml/8fl oz/1 cup water

1 Rinse the chicken under cold water, pat dry, trim off any fat and cut into chunks.

2 Trim and rinse the vegetables and cut into small pieces.

3 Heat the oil in a pan, add the chicken and onion, and fry for a few minutes, stirring until browned. Add the carrots, celery, vegetable purée and water. Bring to the boil, cover and simmer for 20 minutes, until tender.

4 Chop or process the mixture to the desired consistency. If using a food processor, process the solids first and then add the liquid a little at a time.

5 Spoon a little into a bowl, test the temperature and cool if necessary, before giving to the baby.

6 Cover the remaining casserole and transfer to the refrigerator as soon as possible. Use within 24 hours.

• Suitable for freezing.

TIP

For extra flavour, add home-made stock instead of the water, or use commercial stock, but make sure it does not have a high sodium level.

Cauliflower and Broccoli with Cheese

Makes: 600ml/1 pint/2½ cups

175g/6oz cauliflower

175g/6oz broccoli

175g/6oz potato

300ml/½ pint/1¼ cups formula milk

75g/3oz Cheddar or mild cheese

1 Rinse the vegetables, then break the cauliflower and broccoli into florets. Slice the tender stems, but cut out and discard the woody core of the cauliflower. Peel and chop the potatoes into cubes.

2 Place the vegetables and milk in a pan, bring to the boil, cover and simmer for 12–15 minutes, until quite tender.

3 Grate the cheese and add to the vegetables, stirring until the cheese has melted.

4 Process or mash the mixture to the desired consistency, adding a little extra milk if necessary.

5 Spoon a little into a bowl, test the temperature, and cool if necessary, before serving to the baby.

6 Cover the remaining food and transfer to the refrigerator as soon as possible. Use within 24 hours.

- Suitable for freezing.

Tagliatelle and Cheese with Broccoli and Ham

Makes: 600ml/1 pint/2½ cups

115g/4oz broccoli

50g/2oz thinly sliced ham

50g/2oz Cheddar or mild cheese

300ml/½ pint/1¼ cups formula milk

50g/2oz tagliatelle

1 Rinse the broccoli and cut into small florets, chopping the stalks. Chop the ham and grate the Cheddar cheese.

2 Pour the formula milk into a pan, bring to the boil and add the tagliatelle. Simmer uncovered for 5 minutes.

3 Add the broccoli and cook for 10 minutes, until tender.

TIP
Pasta swells on standing, so you may need to thin the cooled leftover mixture with extra formula milk before reheating.

4 Add the ham and cheese to the broccoli and pasta, stirring until the cheese has melted.

5 Chop or process the mixture to the desired consistency and then spoon a little into a bowl. Test the temperature and cool if necessary, before giving to the baby.

6 Cover the remaining food and transfer to the refrigerator as soon as possible. Use within 24 hours.

• Suitable for freezing.

Baby Dahl

Makes: 600ml/1 pint/2½ cups

50g/2oz/¼ cup red lentils

¼ onion

2.5ml/½ tsp ground coriander

1.25ml/¼ tsp turmeric

350ml/12fl oz/1½ cups water

75g/3oz potato

75g/3oz carrot

75g/3oz cauliflower

75g/3oz green cabbage

1 Rinse the lentils under cold water, discarding any black bits.

2 Chop the onion and add to a pan with the lentils, spices and water.

3 Bring to the boil, cover and simmer for 20 minutes.

4 Chop the potato, carrot and cabbage. Break the cauliflower into small florets.

5 Stir the vegetables into the pan. Cook for 12–15 minutes.

6 Chop or process the dahl to the desired consistency, adding a little extra boiled water if necessary.

7 Spoon a little dahl into a bowl, test the temperature and cool if necessary, before serving to the baby.

8 Cover the remaining dahl and transfer to the refrigerator as soon as possible. Use within 24 hours.

• Suitable for freezing.

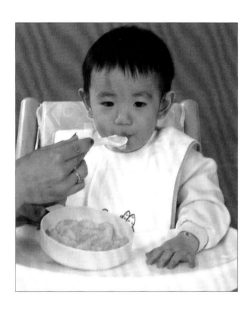

Fish and Cheese Pie

Makes: 450ml/³⁄4 pint/1⁷⁄8 cups

225g/8oz potato

50g/2oz leek

50g/2oz button (white) mushrooms

90g/3½oz brick frozen skinless cod

250ml/8fl oz/1 cup formula milk

50g/2oz grated Cheddar,
  or mild cheese

1 Peel the potato, halve the leek and trim the mushrooms. Place all the vegetables in a colander and rinse well with cold water, drain, then chop the vegetables.

2 Place the vegetables in a pan with the frozen cod and milk. Bring to the boil, cover and simmer for 15 minutes, until the fish is cooked and the potatoes are tender when pierced with a knife.

3 Lift the fish out of the pan with a slotted spoon and break into pieces with a knife and fork, checking carefully for bones.

4 Return the fish to the pan and stir in the grated cheese. Chop or process the mixture to give the desired consistency.

5 Spoon a little into a bowl, test the temperature and cool if necessary, before serving to the baby.

6 Cover the remaining fish pie and transfer to the refrigerator as soon as possible. Use within 24 hours.

• Suitable for freezing.

Fish Creole

Makes: 450ml/³⁄₄ pint/1⁷⁄₈ cups

50g/2oz celery

50g/2oz red (bell) pepper

300ml/½ pint/1¼ cups water

50g/2oz/¼ cup long grain rice

10ml/2 tsp tomato ketchup

90g/3½oz brick frozen skinless cod

1 Trim the celery and discard the core and seeds from the pepper. Rinse and chop the vegetables.

2 Bring the water to the boil in a pan and add the vegetables, rice, ketchup and cod.

3 Bring back to the boil, then reduce heat, cover and simmer for 15 minutes, until the rice is tender and the fish is cooked.

4 Lift the fish out of the pan with a slotted spoon. Use a knife and fork to check for bones.

5 Stir the fish back into the pan and then chop or process.

6 Spoon a little fish mixture into a small bowl, test the temperature and cool if necessary, before giving to the baby.

7 Cover the leftover fish creole and transfer to the refrigerator as soon as possible. Use within 24 hours.

• Suitable for freezing.

Chocolate Pots

Makes: 2

5ml/1 tsp cocoa

5ml/1 tsp caster (superfine) sugar

150ml/¼ pint/⅔ cup formula or
  cow's milk

1 egg

1 Preheat the oven to 180°C/
350°F/Gas 4. Blend the cocoa
and sugar with a little of the milk in a
small bowl to make a smooth paste.
Stir in the remaining milk and then
pour the mixture into a pan.

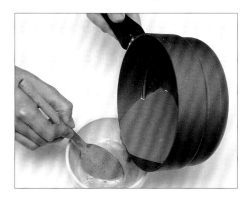

2 Bring just to the boil. Beat the
egg in a bowl, then gradually stir
in the hot milk, mixing well until the
mixture is smooth.

3 Strain the mixture into two
ramekin dishes to remove any
egg solids.

4 Place the dishes in a roasting pan
or shallow cake tin (pan). Pour
boiling water into the pan to come
halfway up the sides of the dishes.

5 Cook in the oven for 15–20
minutes, or until the custard has
set. Leave to cool.

6 Transfer to the refrigerator as soon
as possible. Serve one dessert and
use the second within 24 hours.

Vanilla Custards

Makes: 2

1 egg

5ml/1 tsp caster (superfine) sugar

few drops vanilla essence (extract)

150ml/¼ pint/⅔ cup formula or
  cow's milk

1 Preheat the oven to 180°C/
350°F/Gas 4. Using a fork, beat
the egg, sugar and vanilla essence
together in a bowl.

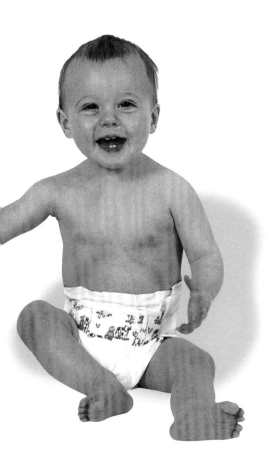

2 Pour the milk into a small pan
and heat until it is just on the
point of boiling.

3 Gradually stir the milk into the
egg mixture, whisking or
beating until smooth.

4 Strain into two ramekin dishes
and place in a roasting pan. Add
enough boiling water to come
halfway up the sides of the dishes.

5 Bake for 15–20 minutes, or until
the custard has set. Cool and
serve as for **Chocolate Pots.**

Marmite Bread Sticks

Makes: 36

little oil, for greasing

150g/5oz packet pizza base mix

flour, for dusting

5ml/1 tsp Marmite (yeast extract spread)

1 egg yolk

1 Brush two baking sheets with a little oil. Put the pizza mix in a bowl, add the quantity of water as directed on the package and mix to make a smooth dough.

2 Knead on a lightly floured surface for 5 minutes, until smooth and elastic.

3 Roll out to a 23cm/9in square. Cut into strips 7.5cm × 1cm/3 × ½in, twisting each to give a corkscrew effect. Arrange on the baking sheets, slightly spaced apart.

4 Mix the Marmite and egg yolk together and brush over the bread sticks. Loosely cover with oiled clear film (plastic wrap) and leave in a warm place for 20–30 minutes to rise.

5 Meanwhile preheat the oven to 220°C/425°F/Gas 7. Bake the bread sticks for 8–10 minutes, until well risen. Loosen but leave to cool on the baking sheet.

6 Serve one or two sticks to the baby. Store the rest in a plastic box for up to three days.

● Suitable for freezing up to three months in a plastic bag.

Bread Fingers with Egg

Makes: 16

2 slices bread

1 egg

30ml/2 tbsp formula or cow's milk

little butter and oil, for frying

1 Trim the crusts off the bread, then cut each slice in half.

2 Beat the egg and milk in a shallow dish and dip the bread, one slice at a time, into the egg until coated on both sides.

3 Heat a little butter and oil in a frying pan. Add the bread and fry until browned on both sides.

4 Cool slightly, cut into fingers and serve to the baby as finger food or as part of a meal.

Cheese Straws

Makes: 42

little oil for greasing

175g/6oz/1½ cups plain (all-purpose) flour

75g/3oz/6 tbsp butter or margarine, cut into pieces

115g/4oz grated Cheddar or mild cheese

1 egg, beaten

1 Preheat the oven to 200°C/ 400°F/Gas 6. Brush two baking sheets lightly with oil.

2 Place the flour in a bowl, add the butter or margarine and rub in until the mixture resembles fine breadcrumbs. Stir in the grated cheese.

3 Reserve 15ml/1 tbsp beaten egg and then stir the rest into the pastry mixture. Mix to a smooth dough, adding water if necessary.

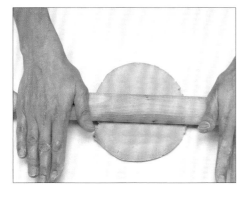

4 Knead lightly and roll out on a floured surface to a rectangle 30 × 20cm/12 × 8in. Brush with the remaining egg.

5 Cut into strips 7.5 × 1cm/ 3 × ½in and place on the baking sheets, spaced slightly apart.

6 Bake in the oven for 8–10 minutes, until golden brown. Loosen from but leave to cool on the baking sheets.

7 Serve one or two sticks to the baby and store the rest in a plastic box for up to 1 week.

● Suitable for freezing up to three months in a plastic box, interleaved with baking parchment.

TIP
Begin making these with mild cheese, and as your child gets more adventurous, change to stronger flavoured cheese.

Mini Cup Cakes

Makes: 26

50g/2oz/4 tbsp soft margarine

50g/2oz/¼ cup caster (superfine) sugar

50g/2oz/⅓ cup self-raising
(self-rising) flour

1 egg

1 Preheat the oven to 180°C/350°F/
Gas 4. Place 26 paper mini muffin
cases on a large baking sheet.

2 Put all the ingredients for the
cake into a mixing bowl and
beat together well until smooth.

3 Divide the mixture among the
cases and cook for 8–10 minutes,
until well risen and golden.

4 Transfer the cakes to a wire rack
and leave to cool completely, then
peel the paper off one or two cakes
and serve to the baby.

5 Store the remaining cakes in a
plastic box for up to three days.

● Suitable for freezing up to three
months in a plastic box.

TIP
Cut a cup cake in half crossways
and spread one half with a little
sugar-free jam. Replace top half
and serve to the baby.

Shortbread Shapes

Makes: 60

little oil, for greasing

150g/5oz/1 cup plain (all-purpose) flour

25g/1oz/3 tbsp cornflour (cornstarch)

50g/2oz/¼ cup caster (superfine) sugar

115g/4oz/½ cup butter

extra sugar, for sprinkling (optional)

1 Preheat the oven to 180°C/ 350°F/Gas 4. Brush two baking sheets with a little oil.

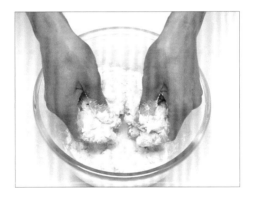

2 Put the flour, cornflour and sugar in a bowl. Cut the butter into pieces and rub into the flour until the mixture resembles fine breadcrumbs. Mould to a dough with your hands.

3 Knead lightly and roll out on a floured surface to a 5mm/¼in thickness. Stamp out shapes with small cookie or petits fours cutters.

4 Transfer to the baking sheets, sprinkle with extra sugar, if liked, and cook for 10–12 minutes, until pale golden. Loosen with a knife and leave to cool on the baking sheets, then transfer to a wire rack.

5 Offer the baby one or two shapes and store the rest in a plastic box for up to one week.

TIP
These biscuits (cookies) will keep well in the freezer for three months. Pack in rigid plastic boxes and thaw in a single layer. If you prefer, you can freeze them before baking. Wrap well to prevent them taking up flavours from other food.

FOOD FOR TODDLERS

Once your child has reached 12 months he or she will be enjoying a varied diet, and eating habits and their personal food preferences will be developing. It is now vitally important to lay the foundations of a good and well-balanced eating regime.

This is a time when food fads may also develop. Try to weather this period of fussy eating – all children will experience it at some time, and even good eaters will go through a picky stage. Hopefully, the fad will go as quickly as it came, but while it lasts, meal-times can become a nightmare.

Coping With a Fussy Eater

We all have different sized appetites whatever our age, and young children are no exception. Children's appetites fluctuate greatly and often tail off just before a growth spurt. All children go through food fads; some just seem to last longer and be more difficult than others.

A toddler's appetite varies enormously, and you may find that she will eat very well one day and eat hardly anything the next. Be guided by your toddler, and try to think in terms of what the child has eaten over several days rather than just concentrating on one day.

At the time, it can be very frustrating and worrying. Try not to think of the food that you have just thrown away, but try to think more in the long term. Jot down the foods that your child has actually eaten over three or four days, or up to a week. You may actually be surprised that it isn't just yogurts and crisps after all!

Once you have a list, you may find a link between the foods your child eats and the time of day. Perhaps your child eats better when eating with the family, or when the house is quiet. If you do find a link, then build on it. You might find that your child is snacking on chocolate, doughnuts or soft drinks when out with friends, and that fussiness at home is really a full tummy. Or it may be that by cutting out a milk drink and a biscuit (cookie) mid-morning and offering a sliced apple instead, your child may not be so full at lunchtime. Perhaps you could hide the biscuit tin (cookie jar) once visitors have had one, so that tiny hands can't keep reaching for more.

If your toddler seems hungrier at breakfast, then you could offer French toast, a grilled sausage or a few banana slices with her cereal.

Above: *Don't panic about food rejection. Be patient and keep a journal listing what your child actually does eat.*

Right: *Fresh, healthy snacks of fruit, such as apples, will preserve your child's appetite for main meals.*

Although this may all sound very obvious, when rushing about caring for a toddler and perhaps an older child or new baby as well, life can become rather blurred, and it can be difficult to stand back and look at things objectively.

REFUSING TO EAT

A child will always eat if she is hungry, although it may not be when you want her to eat. A child can stay fit and healthy on surprisingly little. Providing your child is growing and gaining weight, then don't fuss, but if you are worried, talk to your doctor or health visitor. Take the lead from your child, never force feed a child and try not to let meal-times become a battleground.

MAKING MEAL-TIMES FUN

Coping with a fussy eater can be incredibly frustrating. The less she eats, the crosser you get, and so the spiral goes on as your toddler learns how to control meal-times. To break this vicious circle, try diffusing things by involving your child in the preparation of the meal. You could pack up a picnic with your child's help, choosing together what to take. Then go somewhere different to eat – it could be the back garden, the swings or even the car. Alternatively, have a dollies' or teddies' tea party or make a camp under the dining table or even in the cupboard under the stairs.

Even very young children enjoy having friends round for tea. If your child is going through a fussy or non-eating stage, invite over a little friend with a good appetite. Try to take a back seat, and don't make a fuss over how much the visiting child eats compared to your own.

Above: *Changing the scene and breaking routine can help greatly.*

Below: *Making the meal a special event can distract the child from any eating worries.*

Above: *Getting your child to help you cook the food will encourage her to eat it, too.*

Above: *Children are more likely to eat with friends of their own age around them.*

10 TIPS TO COPE WITH A FUSSY EATER

1 Try to find meals that the rest of the family enjoys and where there are at least one or two things the fussy child will eat, as well. It may seem easier to cook only foods that your child will eat, but it means a very limited diet for everyone else, and your child will never get the chance to have a change of mind and try something new.

2 Serve smaller portions of food to your child.

3 Invite round her friend with a hearty appetite. A good example sometimes works, but don't comment on how much the visiting child has eaten.

4 Invite an adult who the child likes for supper – a granny, uncle or friend. Sometimes a child will eat for someone else without any fuss at all.

5 Never force feed a child.

6 If your child is just playing with the food and won't eat, quietly remove the plate without a fuss and don't offer dessert.

7 Try to make meal-times enjoyable and talk about what the family has been doing.

8 Try limiting snacks and drinks between meals so your child feels hungrier when it comes to family meal-times. Alternatively, offer more nutritious snacks and smaller main meals if your child eats better that way.

9 Offer drinks after a meal so that they don't spoil the appetite.

10 Offer new foods when you know your child is hungry and hopefully more receptive.

Above: *Remember to give drinks after the meal, not before.*

EATING TOGETHER

Sharing meals as a family should be a happy part of the day, but can turn into a nightmare if everyone is tired or you feel as though the only things your children will eat are chips (french fries). There is nothing worse than preparing a lovely supper, laying the table and sitting down with everyone, and then one child refuses to eat, shrieks her disapproval or just pushes the food around the plate. However hard you try to ignore this behaviour, the meal is spoiled for everyone, especially if this is a regular occurrence. It's not fair on you or anyone else.

If you feel this is just a passing phase, then you could try just ignoring it and carry on regardless. Try to praise the good things, perhaps the way the child sits nicely at the table or the way she holds a knife and fork. Talk about the things that have been happening during the day, rather than concentrating on the meal itself. Try to avoid comparing your child's appetite with more hearty eaters. With luck, this particular fad will go away.

However, if it becomes a regular thing and meal-times always seem more like a battleground than a happy family gathering, perhaps it's time for a more serious approach.

First steps

● Check to see if there is something physically wrong with your child. Has she been ill? If she has, she may not have recovered fully. If you're worried, then ask your doctor.
● Perhaps your child has enlarged adenoids or tonsils which could make swallowing difficult, or perhaps she has a food allergy, such as coeliacs disease – an intolerance to gluten, which may be undiagnosed, but which would give the child tummy pains after eating. Again, check with your doctor.
● Is your child worried or stressed? If your family circumstances have changed – the arrival of a new baby, or if you've moved recently – your child may be unhappy or confused.
● Is your child trying to get your attention?

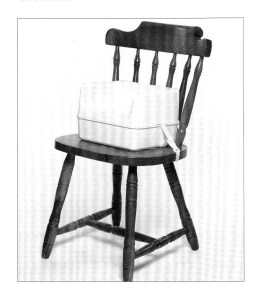

Above: *Good seating of the right height will contribute to comfort and relaxation.*

Secondly
Look at the way in which you as a family eat. Do you eat at regular times? Do you sit down to eat or catch snacks on the move? Do you enjoy your food, or do you always feel rushed and harassed? Children will pick up habits from their parents – bad ones as well as good. If you don't tend to sit down to a meal, or you have the habit of getting up during meal-times to do other jobs, then it's hard to expect your child to behave differently.

Finally
Talk things over with the whole family. If you all feel enough is enough, then it's time to make a plan of action. Explain that from now on you are all going to eat together where possible, when and where you say so. You will choose the food, there will be three meals a day and no snacks. Since milk is filling and dulls the appetite, milky drinks will only be given after a meal; during the meal water or juice will be provided.

It is important to involve the entire family in this strategy so that there is no dipping into the biscuit tin (cookie jar) or raiding the cupboard for crisps (potato chips) after school. Make sure that the fussy eater is aware of what is going to happen and give a few days' notice so that the idea can sink in.

Once you have outlined your strategy, work out your menus and

Happy Families

stick to them. Include foods your child definitely likes, chicken or carrots for instance, and obviously avoid foods your child dislikes although you could introduce some new foods for variety. Set yourself a time scale, perhaps one or two weeks, and review things after this period has elapsed.

PUTTING THE PLAN INTO ACTION
Begin your new plan of action when the entire family is there to help, such as a weekend, and stick to it. Make a fuss of the plans so it seems more like a game than a prison sentence. Add a few flowers to the table or a pretty cloth to make it more special.

Begin the day with a normal breakfast, but give the fussy eater the smallest possible portion. If the child eats it up, then offer something you know your child likes, such as an apple, a few raisins or a fruit yogurt.

As the days progress, you could offer a biscuit (cookie) or milkshake as a treat.

Give plenty of encouragement and praise, but be firm if the child plays up. If she behaves badly, take her to a different room or to the bottom of the stairs and explain that the only food is what is on the table. Sit down with the rest of the family, leaving the fussy eater's food on the table, and try to ignore the child.

If the child changes her mind just as you're about to clear the table, then get the other members of the family to come back and wait until the fussy eater has finished.

Continue in this way with other meals. Don't be swayed if your child says she will eat her food watching TV or if she wants her dessert first. Explain that she must eat just like everyone else or go without.

If she begins to cry, sit her down in another room and return to the table. This is perhaps the hardest thing of all.

After a few days, there should be a glimmer of progress. Still offer tiny portions of food, followed by foods that you know your child will eat as a treat. Keeping to a plan like this is hard, but if the entire family sticks together and thinks positively, then it is possible. Keep to the time span you have decided, then suggest you all go to your local pizza or burger restaurant, and let the fussy eater choose what she likes.

Fat Cat

Veggie Burger

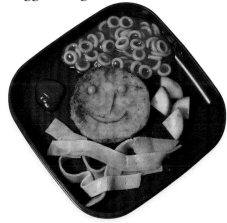

Tuna Fish Cakes

A Balanced and Varied Diet

Give your child a selection of foods in the four main food groups daily:

Cereal and filler foods: include three to four helpings of the following per day – breakfast cereals, bread, pasta, potatoes, rice.

Fruit and vegetables: try to have three or four helpings per day. Choose from fresh, canned, frozen or dried.

Meat and/or alternatives: one to two portions per day – meat (all kinds, including burgers and sausages), poultry, fish (fresh, canned or frozen), eggs (well cooked), lentils, peas and beans (for example, chickpeas baked beans, red kidney beans), finely chopped nuts, smooth peanut butter, seeds, tofu, and Quorn.

Dairy foods: include 600ml/1 pint of milk per day or a mix of milk, cheese, and yogurt. For a child who stops drinking milk, try flavouring it or using it in custards, ice cream, rice pudding or cheese sauce. A carton of yogurt or 40g/1½oz of cheese have the same amount of calcium as 190ml/⅓ pint of milk.

THE IMPORTANCE OF BREAKFAST

Breakfast is a vitally important start for any young child. Count back: your child may have had a meal at 5 o'clock the previous day, and if she misses breakfast at 8 o'clock she will not have eaten for 15 hours. Allow time to sit down, and don't rush your child. Offer milk and cereals, orange juice diluted with a little water, not squash (orangeade), a few slices of fruit and half a piece of toast, preferably spread with smooth peanut butter or Marmite.

Above: *Cereal and filler foods, such as bread, pasta and rice.*

Above: *Fruit and vegetables, including frozen, dried and canned goods.*

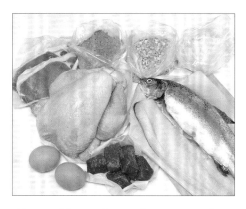

Above: *Meat and meat alternatives, such as beans, peas, lentils and nuts.*

Above: *Dairy foods such as milk, cheese and yogurt.*

Marmite toast

Sliced pears

FATS

As adults we are all aware of the need to cut down on our fat consumption, but when eating together as a family, bear in mind that fat is a useful source of energy in a child's diet. The energy from fat is in concentrated form, so that your child can take in the calories she needs for growth and development before her stomach becomes overfull. Fat in food is also a valuable source of the fat-soluble vitamins, A, D, E and K, as well as essential fatty acids that the body cannot make by itself.

In general, fat is best provided by foods that contain not just fat but other essential nutrients as well, such as dairy products, eggs, meat and fish. Full-fat (whole) milk and its products such as cheese and yogurt, and eggs contain the fat-soluble vitamins A and D, while sunflower (sunflower-seed) oil, nuts and oily fish are a good source of various essential fatty acids.

It is wise to cut down on deep frying and to grill (broil) or oven bake foods where possible. All children love crisps (potato chips), but keep them as a treat rather than a daily snack.

FRUIT AND VEGETABLES

Fresh fruit and vegetables play an essential part in a balanced diet. Offer fresh fruit, such as slices of apple or banana, for breakfast and the evening meal, and perhaps thin sticks of raw carrot and celery for lunch. Instead of biscuits (cookies), offer your child raisins, apricots, satsumas, carrots or apple slices if she wants a mid-morning or afternoon snack. Keep the fruit bowl within easy reach so your child may be tempted to pick up a banana as she walks through the kitchen.

Above: *A good mixture of the four basic food types will provide maximum energy and vitality for growing children.*

SNACKS

Young children cannot eat enough food at meal-times to meet their needs for energy and growth, and snacks can play a vital part in meeting these needs. However, keep biscuits and crisps as a treat. They contain little goodness and are bad for the teeth. At meal-times keep sweets (candy) out of sight until the main course has been eaten.

Above: *Keep sweets and chocolate as treats – give fruit and vegetables as snacks.*

Bread sticks

Raisins

Melon

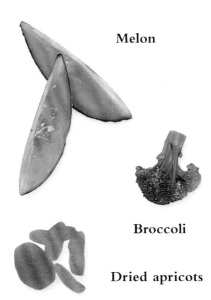

Broccoli

Dried apricots

LUNCH SPECIALS

Now that your baby has progressed from puréed to chopped food, you can begin to cook more grownup lunches. Try to introduce a range of different foods to give a balanced diet and a variety of tastes, but don't be disheartened if there are a few hiccups along the way.

Sticky Chicken

Serves 2–4

4 chicken drumsticks

10ml/2 tsp oil

5ml/1 tsp soy sauce

15ml/1 tbsp smooth peanut butter

15ml/1 tbsp tomato ketchup

small baked potatoes, corn and tomato wedges, to serve

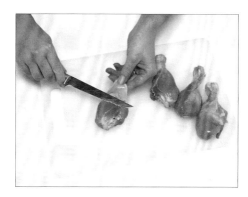

1 Preheat the oven to 200°C/ 400°F/Gas 6 and line a small shallow baking tin (pan) with foil. Rinse the drumsticks under cold water, pat dry and peel off the skin. Make three or four slashes in the meat with a sharp knife and place in the tin.

TIP

If more convenient, use the peanut butter and ketchup mixture over chicken thighs or kebabs instead.

2 Blend the remaining ingredients and spread thickly over the top of the chicken drumsticks. Cook in the oven for 15 minutes.

3 Turn the drumsticks over and baste with the peanut butter mixture and meat juices.

4 Cook for a further 20 minutes or until the juices run clear when the chicken is pierced with a knife.

5 Cool slightly, then wrap a small piece of foil around the base of each drumstick. Arrange on plates and serve with small baked potatoes, hot corn, and tomato wedges.

Coriander Chicken Casserole

Serves 2

2 chicken thighs

¼ small onion

1 small carrot, about 50g/2oz

50g/2oz swede (rutabaga)

5ml/1 tsp oil

2.5ml/½ tsp ground coriander

pinch of turmeric

5ml/1 tsp plain (all-purpose) flour

150ml/¼ pint/⅔ cup chicken stock

salt and pepper (optional)

mashed potatoes and peas, to serve

1 Preheat the oven to 180°C/ 350°F/Gas 4. Rinse the chicken under cold water, pat dry and trim away any excess skin if necessary. Chop the onion, carrot and swede.

2 Heat the oil in a frying pan, add the chicken and brown on each side. Add the vegetables.

TIP

Chop the meat for very young toddlers. Serve older children the whole thigh to make them feel more grown up, then help with cutting.

3 Stir in the coriander, turmeric and flour, then add the stock and a little salt and pepper, if liked. Bring to the boil, then transfer to a casserole.

4 Cover and cook in the oven for 1 hour. Spoon on to serving plates or into shallow dishes, cool slightly and serve the chicken casserole with mashed potatoes and peas.

Chicken and Cheese Parcels

Serves 2

1 boned and skinned chicken breast, about 150g/5oz

25g/1oz Cheddar or mild cheese

1 slice lean ham, cut into 4 strips

15ml/1 tbsp oil

new potatoes, broccoli and carrots, to serve

1 Rinse the chicken under cold water, pat dry with kitchen paper and cut in half crossways. Place each half between two pieces of clear film (plastic wrap) and flatten with a rolling pin until each piece is about 10cm/4in square.

2 Cut the cheese in half and place a piece on each escalope (US scallop). Wrap the chicken around the cheese to enclose it completely.

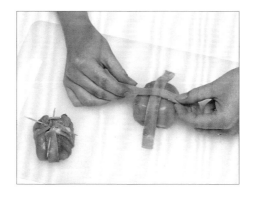

3 Arrange two pieces of the ham crossways over each of the parcels, securing them underneath with cocktail sticks (toothpicks). Brush the chicken parcels with oil.

TIP

You could wrap the parcels with halved rashers (strips) of rindless streaky (fatty) bacon, if preferred.

4 Place on a piece of foil and chill until ready to cook.

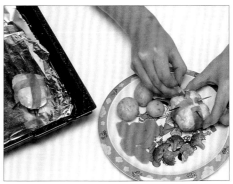

5 Preheat the grill (broiler). Cook the chicken for 10 minutes, turning once, until browned. Remove the cocktail sticks, cool slightly, then arrange on two plates and serve with new potatoes, steamed broccoli florets and sliced carrots.

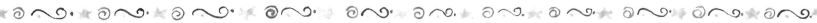

Peppered Beef Casserole

Serves 2

115g/4oz lean braising steak

¼ small onion

¼ small red (bell) pepper

¼ small yellow (bell) pepper

5ml/1 tsp oil

30ml/2 tbsp canned red kidney
  beans, drained and rinsed

5ml/1 tsp plain (all-purpose) flour

150ml/¼ pint/⅔ cup lamb stock

15ml/1 tbsp tomato ketchup

5ml/1 tsp Worcestershire sauce

45ml/3 tbsp couscous

a few drops of oil

40g/1½oz/3 tbsp frozen peas

salt and pepper (optional)

1 Preheat the oven to 180°C/
350°F/Gas 4. Rinse the meat
under cold water and pat dry. Trim
away any fat and cut into small cubes.

2 Chop the onion, remove the seeds
and core from the peppers and cut
into small cubes.

3 Heat the oil in a pan, add the beef
and onion and fry gently until
browned, stirring frequently.

4 Add the peppers and kidney beans,
then stir in the flour, stock, tomato
ketchup, Worcestershire sauce and a
little salt and pepper if liked.

5 Bring to the boil, stirring, then
transfer to a casserole dish, cover
and cook in the oven for about 1½
hours, or until the meat is tender.

6 Just before serving place the
couscous in a bowl, cover with
boiling water and leave to soak for
5 minutes. Drain into a sieve (strainer)
and stir in a few drops of oil.

7 Bring a pan of water to the boil,
add the peas, and place the sieve of
couscous over the pan. Cover and
cook for 5 minutes.

8 Spoon the casserole on to two
plates or dishes. Fluff up the
couscous with a fork, drain the peas
and spoon on to the plates. Cool
slightly before serving.

Lamb Stew

Serves 2

115g/4oz lamb fillet

¼ small onion

1 small carrot, about 50g/2oz

½ small parsnip, about 50g/2oz

1 small potato

5ml/1 tsp oil

150ml/¼ pint/⅔ cup lamb stock

pinch of dried rosemary

salt and pepper (optional)

crusty bread, to serve

1 Rinse the lamb under cold water and pat dry. Cut away any fat from the meat and cut into small cubes. Finely chop the onion, then dice the carrot and parsnip and cut the potato into slightly larger pieces.

2 Heat the oil in a medium-size pan, add the lamb and onion, and fry gently until browned. Add the carrot, parsnip and potato, and fry the lamb and vegetables for a further 3 minutes, stirring.

3 Add the lamb stock, dried rosemary and a little salt and pepper, if liked. Bring to the boil, cover and simmer for 35–40 minutes, or until the meat is tender and moist.

4 Spoon the stew into shallow bowls and cool slightly before serving with crusty bread.

Mexican Beef

Serves 3–4

¼ small onion

1 strip red (bell) pepper

½ small courgette (zucchini)

115g/4oz lean minced (ground) beef

1 small garlic clove, crushed

45ml/3 tbsp canned baked beans

45ml/3 tbsp beef stock

15ml/1 tbsp tomato ketchup

18 corn chips

25g/1oz/¼ cup grated Cheddar or
  mild cheese

green salad, to serve

1 Finely chop the onion and dice
the pepper and courgette.

2 Dry fry the onion and meat in a
medium-size pan, stirring until
browned all over.

3 Stir in the remaining ingredients
and bring to the boil, stirring.
Cover and simmer the mixture for
15 minutes, stirring occasionally.

4 Place the corn chips on plates,
spoon on the mixture and
sprinkle the grated cheese over the
top. Serve with a green salad.

Lamb and Celery Casserole

Serves 2

115g/4oz lamb fillet

¼ onion

1 small carrot, about 50g/2oz

1 celery stick

25g/1oz button (white) mushrooms

5ml/1 tsp oil

bay leaf

10ml/2 tsp plain (all-purpose) flour

175ml/6fl oz/¾ cup lamb stock

salt and pepper (optional)

mashed potatoes and baby Brussels
  sprouts, to serve

1 Preheat the oven to 180°C/
350°F/Gas 4. Rinse the lamb
under cold water and pat dry, then
trim off any fat and cut into small
cubes. Chop the onion and carrot,
rinse the celery and mushrooms, pat
dry and slice thinly.

2 Heat the oil in a frying pan, add
the lamb, onion and bay leaf and
fry gently until the lamb is browned,
stirring frequently. Add the remaining
vegetables and fry for a further
3 minutes, until they are softened
and lightly browned.

VARIATION
For a more unusual flavour,
substitute fennel for the celery.
Its slight aniseed taste goes well
with lamb.

3 Stir in the flour, then add the
stock, and a little salt and
pepper, if liked. Bring to the boil
and then transfer to a casserole,
cover and cook in the oven for 45
minutes or until the meat is tender.

4 Spoon the casserole on to plates,
discarding the bay leaf. Cool
slightly, then serve with mashed
potatoes and tiny Brussels sprouts.

Shepherd's Pie

Serves 2

½ small onion

175g/6oz lean minced (ground)
  beef

10ml/2 tsp plain (all-purpose) flour

30ml/2 tbsp tomato ketchup

150ml/¼ pint/⅔ cup beef stock

pinch of mixed herbs

50g/2oz swede (rutabaga)

½ small parsnip, about 50g/2oz

1 medium potato, about 115g/4oz

10ml/2 tsp milk

15g/½oz/1 tbsp butter or margarine

½ carrot

40g/1½oz/3 tbsp frozen peas

salt and pepper (optional)

1 Preheat oven to 190°C/375°F/
Gas 5. Finely chop the onion,
and place in a small pan with
the mince and dry fry over a low
heat, stirring, until the mince is
evenly browned.

5 Spoon the meat into two
250ml/8fl oz/1 cup ovenproof
dishes. Place the mashed vegetables
on top, fluffing them up with a fork.
Dot with butter or margarine.

6 Place both the pies on a baking
sheet and cook for 25–30 minutes,
until browned on top and bubbly.

7 Peel and thinly slice the carrot
lengthways. Stamp out shapes
with petits fours cutters. Cook in a
pan of boiling water with the peas for
5 minutes. Drain and serve with the
shepherd's pies. Remember that baked
pies are very hot when they come out
of the oven. Always allow to cool
slightly before serving to children.

2 Add the flour, stirring, then add
the ketchup, stock, mixed herbs
and seasoning, if liked. Bring to the
boil, cover and simmer gently for
30 minutes, stirring occasionally.

3 Meanwhile, chop the swede,
parsnip and potato, and cook for
20 minutes, until tender. Drain.

4 Mash with the milk and half of
the butter or margarine.

Tuna Fish Cakes

Serves 2–3

1 large potato, about 225g/8oz

knob (pat) of butter or margarine

10ml/2 tsp milk

5ml/1 tsp lemon juice

100g/3½oz can tuna fish

40g/1½oz/3 tbsp frozen corn, defrosted

flour, for dusting

1 egg

60ml/4 tbsp ground almonds

50g/2oz green beans

½ carrot

6 frozen peas

15ml/1 tbsp oil

salt and pepper (optional)

1 Peel and cut the potato into chunks and then cook in a pan of boiling water for about 15 minutes until tender. Drain and mash with the butter or margarine and milk.

2 Add the lemon juice and a little salt and pepper, if liked. Drain the tuna fish and stir into the potato with the defrosted corn.

3 Divide the mixture into six and pat each portion into a fish shape with floured hands.

4 Beat the egg in a dish and place the ground almonds on a plate. Dip the fish cakes into the egg and then into the almonds, making sure they are completely covered. Place on a floured plate and chill until ready to cook.

5 Trim the beans, and peel and cut the carrot into sticks a little smaller than the beans. Cook in a pan of boiling water with the peas for about 5 minutes.

6 Meanwhile heat the oil in a frying pan, and fry the fish cakes for 5 minutes, until golden brown and crisp, turning once.

7 Drain and arrange on serving plates with pea "eyes" and bean and carrot "pond weed". Cool slightly before serving.

Fish and Cheese Pies

Serves 2

1 medium potato, about 150g/5oz
25g/1oz green cabbage
115g/4oz cod or hoki fillets
25g/1oz/2 tbsp frozen corn
150ml/¼ pint/⅔ cup milk
15ml/1 tbsp butter or margarine
15ml/1 tbsp plain (all-purpose) flour
25g/1oz/¼ cup grated Red Leicester or mild cheese
5ml/1 tsp sesame seeds
carrots and mangetouts (snowpeas), to serve

4 Strain the fish and corn, reserving the cooking liquid. Wash the pan, then melt the butter or margarine in the pan. Stir in the flour, then gradually add the reserved cooking liquid and bring to the boil, stirring until thickened and smooth.

5 Add the fish and corn with half of the grated cheese. Spoon into two small ovenproof dishes.

6 Mash the potato and cabbage with the remaining 10ml/2 tsp milk. Stir in half of the remaining cheese and spoon the mixture over the fish. Sprinkle with the sesame seeds and the remaining cheese.

7 Cook under a preheated grill until the topping is browned. Cool slightly before serving with carrot and mangetout vegetable fishes.

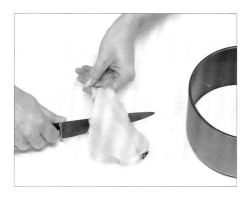

1 Peel and cut the potato into chunks and shred the cabbage. Cut any skin away from the fish fillets and rinse under cold water.

2 Bring a pan of water to the boil, add the potato and cook for 10 minutes. Add the cabbage and cook for a further 5 minutes until tender. Drain.

3 Meanwhile, place the fish fillets, the corn and all but 10ml/2 tsp of the milk in a second pan. Bring to the boil, then cover the pan and simmer very gently for 8–10 minutes, until the fish flakes easily when pressed with a knife.

Surprise Fish Parcels

Serves 2

½ small courgette (zucchini)

175g/6oz smoked haddock or cod

1 small tomato

knob (pat) of butter or margarine

pinch of dried mixed herbs

new potatoes and broccoli, to serve

1 Preheat the oven to 200°C/
400°F/Gas 6. Tear off two pieces
of foil, then trim and thinly slice the
courgette and divide equally
between the two pieces of foil.

2 Cut the skin away from the fish,
remove any bones, cut into two
equal pieces and rinse under cold
water. Pat the haddock dry and place
on top of the courgettes.

3 Slice the tomato and arrange
slices on top of each piece of
haddock. Add a little butter or
margarine to each and sprinkle with
mixed herbs.

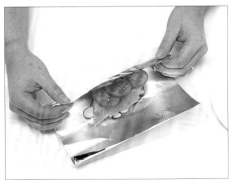

4 Wrap the foil around the fish and
seal the edges of each piece to
make two parcels, then place the
parcels on a baking sheet and cook
in the oven for 15–20 minutes,
depending on the thickness of the fish.

5 To test if they are cooked, open
up one of the parcels and insert a
knife into the centre. If the fish flakes
easily, then it is ready.

6 Cool slightly, then arrange the
parcels on plates and serve with
new potatoes and broccoli.

Cowboy Sausages and Beans

Serves 2

3 chipolata sausages

¼ small onion

1 small carrot, about 50g/2oz

1 strip red (bell) pepper

5ml/1 tsp oil

200g/7oz can baked beans

10ml/2 tsp Worcestershire sauce

fingers of toast, to serve

1 Press the centre of each sausage, twist and cut in half to make two small sausages.

2 Finely chop the onion, then dice the carrot and the pepper, discarding the core and seeds.

3 Heat the oil in a frying pan, add the sausages and the chopped onion and fry until browned.

TIP
Check the beans towards the end of cooking – you may need to add a little extra water.

4 Add the remaining ingredients and stir in 30ml/2 tbsp water. Cover and cook for 15 minutes, or until the carrot is cooked.

5 Spoon on to serving plates or into dishes, cool slightly and serve with fingers of toast.

Mini Toad-in-the-Hole

Serves 2

3 chipolata sausages

5ml/1 tsp oil

60ml/4 tbsp plain (all-purpose) flour

1 egg

60ml/4 tbsp milk

salt

baked beans and green beans, to serve

1 Preheat the oven to 220°C/ 425°F/Gas 7. Press the centre of each sausage with your finger, twist and then cut in half. Brush two 10cm/4in tartlet tins (muffin pans) with oil. Add the sausages and cook for about 5 minutes.

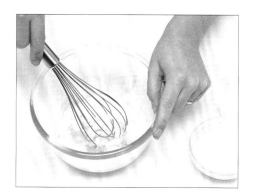

2 Place the flour, egg and a pinch of salt in a bowl. Gradually whisk in the milk, beating until a smooth batter is formed.

3 Pour into the tins, quickly return to the oven and bake for 15 minutes, until risen and golden.

4 Loosen with a knife and turn out on to serving plates. Cool slightly and serve with baked beans and steamed green beans.

Pork Hotpot

Serves 2

175g/6oz lean pork

¼ small onion

5ml/1 tsp oil

5ml/1 tsp plain (all-purpose) flour

40g/1½oz/3 tbsp frozen corn

pinch of dried sage

150ml/¼ pint/⅔ cup chicken stock

1 medium potato, about 150g/5oz

1 carrot, about 75g/3oz

knob (pat) of butter or margarine

salt and pepper (optional)

broccoli and Brussels sprouts,
  to serve

1 Preheat the oven to 180°C/
350°F/Gas 4. Rinse the pork
under cold water, pat dry, trim away
any fat and cut into small cubes. Peel
and finely chop the onion.

2 Heat the oil in a frying pan, add
the cubed pork and onion and
fry until golden brown, stirring.

3 Add in the flour and stir until
blended, then add the corn, dried
sage, stock and a little salt and pepper,
if liked. Bring to the boil and then
turn the mixture into a shallow
ovenproof dish.

4 Peel and thinly slice the potato
and carrot. Arrange slices so that
they overlap on top of the pork
mixture. Dot with butter or
margarine. Cover with foil and cook
in the oven for about 1 hour, until the
potatoes are tender.

5 Remove the foil and brown
under the grill (broiler) if liked.
Spoon on to serving plates, cool
slightly, then serve with steamed
broccoli and Brussels sprouts.

TIP

If you are cooking for only one
child, make the hotpot in two
dishes. Cool one, cover with clear
film (plastic wrap) and freeze for
up to three months.

Pork and Lentil Casserole

Serves 2

175g/6oz boneless spare-rib pork chop

¼ small onion

1 small carrot, about 50g/2oz

5ml/1 tsp oil

1 small garlic clove, crushed

25g/1oz red lentils

90ml/6 tbsp canned chopped tomatoes

90ml/6 tbsp chicken stock

salt and pepper (optional)

swede (rutabaga) and peas, to serve

1 Preheat the oven to 180°C/ 350°F/Gas 4. Trim off any excess fat from the pork and cut in half. Finely chop the onion and dice the carrot.

2 Heat the oil in a frying pan, add the pork and onion and fry until the pork is browned on both sides.

3 Add the garlic, lentils and carrots and stir gently to mix.

4 Pour in the chopped tomatoes, stock and seasoning, if liked, and cook briefly to bring to the boil. Transfer to a casserole, cover and cook in the oven for 1¼ hours.

5 Spoon portions on to serving plates or shallow dishes and cool slightly. Serve with diced buttered swede and peas.

TIP

Teaching a child to use a knife and fork can be frustrating. Spare-rib pork chops are wonderfully tender when casseroled and so very easy to cut with a child's knife.

Sticky Ribs and Apple Slaw

Serves 2

225g/8oz short pork ribs

10ml/2 tsp oil

10ml/2 tsp tomato ketchup

10ml/2 tsp hoisin sauce

1 medium potato, scrubbed but not peeled

knob (pat) of butter or margarine

For the Apple Slaw

½ carrot

½ eating apple

25g/1oz white cabbage

10ml/2 tsp sultanas (golden raisins)

30ml/2 tbsp mayonnaise

carrot slices, tomato wedges and celery sticks, to serve

4 Meanwhile peel the carrot, and peel, quarter and core the apple. Coarsely grate the apple and carrot and finely chop the cabbage.

5 Place in a bowl with the sultanas and mayonnaise and mix well.

6 Arrange the ribs on serving plates. Halve the baked potato, add a little butter or margarine to each half and serve with the pork ribs, together with star-shaped carrot slices, celery sticks and tomato wedges and spoonfuls of coleslaw.

TIP

Check the temperature of the ribs before serving, as they stay very hot for a surprisingly long time. Nothing will put a child off more than food that is very hot. Toddlers prefer their food to be lukewarm.

1 Preheat the oven to 200°C/ 400°F/Gas 6. Rinse the pork ribs under cold water, pat dry and put on a roasting rack set over a small roasting pan. Mix the oil, ketchup and hoisin sauce, and brush over the ribs, reserving any extra mixture.

2 Pour a little boiling water into the base of the roasting pan. Prick the potato all over with a fork and then place in the oven with the spare ribs, preferably on the same shelf.

3 Cook for 1 hour, turning the pork ribs once during cooking and brushing with any of the remaining ketchup mixture.

Mini Cheese and Ham Tarts

Makes 12

For the Pastry

115g/4oz/1 cup plain (all-purpose) flour

50g/2oz/4 tbsp margarine

For the Filling

50g/2oz/½ cup mild cheese

2 thin slices ham, chopped

75g/3oz/½ cup frozen corn

1 egg

120ml/4fl oz/½ cup milk

pinch of paprika

salt and pepper

carrot and cucumber sticks, to serve

1 Preheat the oven to 200°C/400°F/ Gas 6. Place the flour in a bowl, add the margarine and rub in with your fingertips until the mixture resembles fine breadcrumbs.

2 Stir in 20ml/4 tsp water and mix to a smooth dough. Lightly knead and roll out on a floured surface.

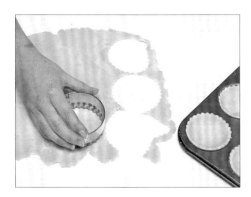

3 Stamp out twelve 7.5cm/3in circles with a fluted cookie cutter, re-rolling the pastry as necessary. Press into a tartlet tin (muffin pan).

TIP
Encourage children to eat more vegetables by serving them with a yogurt dip flavoured with tomato purée (paste).

4 Grate the cheese, mix with the ham and corn, and divide among the pastry cases.

5 Beat together the egg, milk, salt and pepper and pour into the tarts. Sprinkle with paprika.

6 Cook in the oven for 12–15 minutes, until well risen and browned. Serve warm with carrot and cucumber sticks.

GOING GREEN

GETTING CHILDREN TO EAT MORE THAN A FEW FROZEN PEAS AND THE ODD CARROT CAN BE AN UPHILL BATTLE. ENCOURAGE THEM TO BE A LITTLE MORE ADVENTUROUS BY MIXING THEIR FAVOURITE FOODS WITH SOME NEW VEGETABLES.

Pick-up Sticks

Serves 2

5cm/2in piece of leek

25g/1oz green beans

1 strip red (bell) pepper

1 celery stick

25g/1oz beansprouts

1 small carrot, about 50g/2oz

5ml/1 tsp oil

15ml/1 tbsp tomato ketchup

5ml/1 tsp soy sauce

pinch ground ginger

grilled (broiled) sausages, to serve

1 Rinse the leek, beans, pepper, celery and beansprouts. Peel the carrot. Halve any large beans and beansprouts. Cut the remaining vegetables into thin strips.

2 Heat the oil in a frying pan, add all the vegetables except the beansprouts and fry for 3 minutes, stirring all the time.

3 Add the beansprouts, ketchup, soy sauce, ginger and 10ml/2 tsp water. Cook for a further 2 minutes, stirring until the vegetables are hot.

4 Spoon on to serving plates and leave to cool slightly. Serve with grilled sausages.

TIP
Don't overcook the vegetables. They should be quite crisp, and firm enough for your child to pick up.

Spinach Pancakes with Ham and Cheese

Serves 2–3

50g/2oz fresh spinach, leaves only

50g/2oz plain (all-purpose) flour

1 egg yolk

300ml/½ pint/1¼ cups milk

15ml/1 tbsp oil

For the Filling

15ml/1 tbsp margarine

15ml/1 tbsp plain (all-purpose) flour

25g/1oz/¼ cup grated Red Leicester
   or mild cheese

40g/1½oz thinly sliced ham, chopped

40g/1½oz button (white) mushrooms,
   thinly sliced

1 Wash the spinach leaves well in cold water and then place in a frying pan, set over a medium heat. Cover and cook gently for 2–3 minutes, until the spinach has just wilted, stirring occasionally. Drain off any excess liquid and cool.

2 Put the flour, egg yolk and a little salt and pepper, if liked, into a bowl. Whisk in half of the milk to make a smooth batter. Finely chop the spinach and stir into the batter.

5 Continue making pancakes until all the batter is used up.

6 Fold the pancakes into quarters, then spoon a little of the ham mixture into each one. Arrange the pancakes on plates and serve with tomato wedges and new potatoes.

3 Melt the margarine in a pan, stir in the flour and then gradually stir in the remaining milk and bring to the boil, stirring continuously until smooth. Add the cheese, ham and mushrooms and stir to mix. Heat, cover and keep warm.

4 Heat a little oil in a frying pan, pour off excess, then add 30ml/ 2 tbsp pancake batter, tilting the pan so that the batter covers the base. Cook for a few minutes until browned, then flip over and cook the other side until golden. Slide the pancake on to a plate and keep warm.

TIP
If offering spinach to your child for the first time, make sure that the filling includes foods that you know are liked. Omit or add ingredients as necessary.

Cauliflower and Broccoli with Cheese

Serves 2

1 egg

75g/3oz cauliflower

75g/3oz broccoli

15g/½oz/1 tbsp margarine

15ml/1 tbsp plain (all-purpose) flour

150ml/¼ pint/⅔ cup milk

40g/1½oz/⅓ cup grated Red
  Leicester or mild cheese

½ tomato

salt and pepper (optional)

1 Put the egg in a small pan of cold water, bring to the boil and cook for about 10 minutes until the egg is hard-boiled.

2 Meanwhile, cut the cauliflower and broccoli into florets and thinly slice the broccoli stalks. Cook in a pan of boiling water for about 8 minutes, until just tender.

3 Drain the vegetables and dry the pan. Melt the margarine, stir in the flour, then gradually mix in the milk and bring to the boil, stirring until thickened and smooth.

TIP
Making a face or fun pattern can be just enough to tempt a fussy eater to try something new.

4 Stir two-thirds of the cheese into the sauce together with a little seasoning, if liked. Reserve two of the broccoli florets and stir the remaining vegetables into the sauce.

5 Divide the mixture between two heat-resistant shallow dishes and sprinkle with the remaining cheese.

6 Place under a hot grill (broiler) until golden brown and bubbling.

7 Make a face on each dish with broccoli florets for a nose, a halved tomato for a mouth and peeled and sliced hard-boiled egg for eyes. Cool slightly before serving.

Potato Boats

Serves 2

2 small baking potatoes
5cm/2in piece leek
25g/1oz button (white) mushrooms
10ml/2 tsp oil
25g/1oz/2 tbsp frozen corn
15ml/1 tbsp milk
knob (pat) of butter
½ small courgette (zucchini), grated
1 carrot, about 50g/2oz, grated
2 slices processed cheese
1 slice ham
salt and pepper (optional)

1 Preheat the oven to 200°C/ 400°F/Gas 6. Prick the potatoes with a fork and bake for 1 hour, until soft. Alternatively, prick well and then microwave on a sheet of kitchen paper on High (full power) for 7–8 minutes.

2 Halve the leek lengthways, wash thoroughly to remove any grit and then slice thinly. Rinse the mushrooms, pat dry and thinly slice.

3 Heat 5ml/1 tsp oil in a frying pan and gently fry the leek, mushrooms and corn for about 3 minutes, until softened, stirring frequently. Turn into a bowl and keep warm.

4 When the potatoes are cooked, cut in half and scoop the centres into the bowl with the leek and mushroom mixture. Add the milk, butter and a little salt and pepper if liked, and stir to mix. Pile the mixture back into the potato shells.

5 Reheat the remaining 5ml/1 tsp of oil and fry the grated courgette and carrot for 2 minutes, until softened. Spoon on to two small plates and spread with a fork to cover the bases of the plates.

6 Arrange two potato halves on each plate. For sails, cut the cheese and ham into triangles and secure to potatoes with cocktail sticks. Cool slightly before serving.

Fat Cats

Serves 2

oil, for greasing

200g/7oz frozen puff pastry, defrosted

a little flour, for dusting

beaten egg, to glaze

50g/2oz broccoli

25g/1oz/2 tbsp frozen mixed vegetables

15ml/1 tbsp butter or margarine

15ml/1 tbsp plain (all-purpose) flour

100ml/3½fl oz/½ cup milk

30ml/2 tbsp grated Cheddar or mild cheese

a little mustard and cress (fine curled cress), to garnish

1 Preheat the oven to 220°C/ 425°F/Gas 7 and lightly brush a baking sheet with a little oil. Roll out the pastry thinly on a surface lightly dusted with a little flour.

2 Using a shaped cookie cutter, stamp out four 13cm/5in cat shapes. Place two cats on the baking sheet and brush with egg.

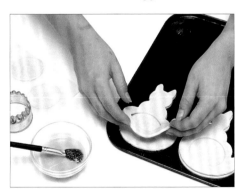

3 Cut a large hole in the centres of the two remaining cats and place the shapes on top of the other two cats.

VARIATION
Ring the changes by making this recipe using different shaped cookie cutters for the pastry shapes. Get your child to choose his favourite.

4 Brush the tops with egg and cook for 10 minutes, until the pastry is well risen and golden.

5 Meanwhile chop the broccoli and cook in a small pan of boiling water with the frozen vegetables for 5 minutes. Drain.

6 Dry the pan and melt the butter or margarine. Stir in the flour and then gradually add the milk. Bring to the boil, stirring all the time until thickened and smooth.

7 Reserve two peas, two pieces of carrot, and two pieces of red bell pepper. Stir the remaining vegetables into the sauce with the grated cheese.

8 Enlarge the cavity in the centre of each pastry cat by scooping out a little of the pastry. Spoon in the vegetable mixture and arrange on two serving plates. Garnish with halved peas for eyes, halved carrot strips for whiskers and red pepper noses. Add mustard and cress. Cool slightly before serving.

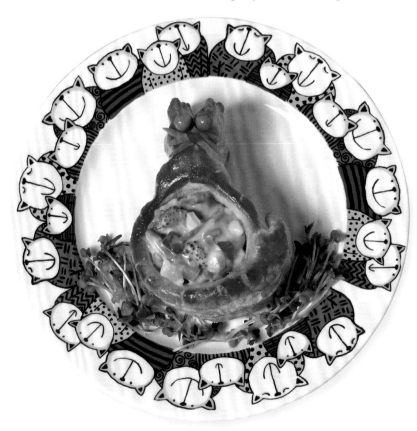

Potato, Carrot and Courgette Rösti

Serves 2–4

1 small potato, about 115g/4oz

½ carrot, about 25g/1oz

½ courgette (zucchini), about 25g/1oz

10ml/2 tsp vegetable oil

sausages and baked beans, to serve

1 Grate the potato, carrot and courgette into a bowl and mix together thoroughly.

2 Place several sheets of kitchen paper on a surface and put the vegetables on top. Cover with more kitchen paper and press down to soak up all the excess liquid.

3 Heat the oil in a frying pan and spoon the vegetables into the pan to form eight rounds. Flatten slightly with a fork and fry four of the rounds for 5 minutes, turning once until the potatoes are thoroughly cooked and the rösti is golden brown on both sides.

4 Lift out of the pan and cook the remaining mixture. Cool slightly and serve with grilled sausages and baked beans.

Veggie Burgers

Serves 2–4

1 large or 2 small potatoes, about 225g/8oz

1 carrot, about 50g/2oz

25g/1oz broccoli

25g/1oz Brussels sprouts

1 egg yolk

15ml/1 tbsp plain (all-purpose) flour

15ml/1 tbsp freshly grated Parmesan cheese

15ml/1 tbsp oil

salt and pepper (optional)

canned spaghetti hoops, strips of ham, wedges of cucumber, and tomato ketchup, to serve

1 Cut the potato and carrot into chunks and cook in boiling water for 15 minutes, until tender.

2 Meanwhile, cut the broccoli into small florets, chop the stem finely and thinly slice the Brussels sprouts. Rinse under cold water then add to the potatoes and carrots for the last 5 minutes of cooking.

3 Drain the vegetables thoroughly and then mash together. Add the egg yolk, and a little salt and pepper, if liked, then mix well.

4 Divide into four and shape into burgers with floured hands. Coat in flour and Parmesan cheese.

5 Heat the oil in a frying pan, add the burgers and fry for 5 minutes, turning once until golden brown. Cool slightly, then serve with canned spaghetti hoops, strips of ham, a few cucumber wedges and a little tomato ketchup. Add a face with peas, carrot and cucumber.

TIP
To make a spider, add cooked green bean legs, a red (bell) pepper mouth and yellow pepper eyes.

Vegetable Lasagne

Serves 2–3

¼ small onion

50g/2oz carrot

50g/2oz courgette (zucchini)

50g/2oz aubergine (eggplant)

25g/1oz button (white) mushrooms

10ml/2 tsp oil

1 small garlic clove, crushed

225g/8oz can chopped tomatoes

pinch of mixed herbs

15ml/1 tbsp butter or margarine

15ml/1 tbsp plain (all-purpose) flour

150ml/¼ pint/⅔ cup milk

60ml/4 tbsp grated mild cheese

3 sheets pre-cooked lasagne

salt and pepper

mixed salad, to serve

1 Finely chop the onion and carrot, and finely dice the courgette and aubergine. Wipe and thinly slice the mushrooms.

2 Heat the oil and fry the vegetables for 3 minutes until softened. Add the garlic, tomatoes and herbs, then bring to the boil, cover and simmer for 5 minutes.

3 Melt the butter or margarine in a pan, stir in the flour. Add the milk and bring to the boil, stirring, until thickened. Stir in half of the grated cheese and a little salt and pepper.

4 Preheat the oven to 180°C/350°F/Gas 4. Spoon one-third of the vegetable mixture into the base of an ovenproof dish, then add a little sauce. Add a slice of lasagne, then cover with half of the remaining vegetable mixture and half the remaining sauce.

5 Add a second sheet of pasta and top with the remaining vegetable mixture. Add a third sheet of lasagne and top with the remaining cheese sauce. Sprinkle with the remaining cheese.

6 Cook for 50–60 minutes, checking after 30 minutes and covering loosely with foil if the topping is browning too quickly. Spoon on to serving plates and leave the lasagne to cool slightly. Serve with a little mixed salad.

Aubergine Bolognese

Serves 2

50g/2oz aubergine (eggplant)

1 strip red (bell) pepper

1 strip yellow (bell) pepper

5cm/2in piece of leek

1 carrot, about 50g/2oz

10ml/2 tsp oil

1 small garlic clove, crushed

25g/1oz/2 tbsp frozen corn

25g/1oz/2 tbsp red lentils

225g/8oz can chopped tomatoes

250ml/8fl oz/1 cup vegetable stock

pinch of dried herbs

50g/2oz dried pasta shapes

knob (pat) of butter or margarine

30ml/2 tbsp grated cheese (optional)

salt and pepper

1 Rinse the aubergine, peppers and leek, peel the carrot and then finely dice all the vegetables.

2 Heat the oil in a medium-size pan, add the diced vegetables and gently fry for 3 minutes, stirring frequently, until slightly softened.

TIP

Sprinkle the diced aubergine with salt, leave to drain in a colander for 30 minutes, then rinse. This removes any bitter taste.

3 Add the garlic, corn, lentils, tomatoes, stock, herbs and a little salt and pepper.

4 Bring to the boil, cover and simmer for about 30 minutes, stirring occasionally and adding a little extra stock if necessary.

5 In the last 10 minutes of cooking, bring a pan of water to the boil and add the pasta. Cook for 10 minutes, until tender.

6 Drain, toss in a little butter or margarine. Spoon on to plates and top with the aubergine bolognese. Sprinkle with cheese.

Quick Meals

If you've had a busy day, rustle up these quick and tasty toddlers' meals – they all cook in 10 minutes or less, and there is a wide variety of recipes to choose from. Remember the importance of fun presentation, to tempt your toddler to try new foods.

Speedy Chicken Pie

Serves 2

1 celery stick

25g/1oz/2 tbsp frozen corn, defrosted

30ml/2 tbsp mayonnaise

2.5ml/½ tsp ground coriander

75g/3oz cold cooked chicken

½ small packet plain crisps (US potato chips)

15ml/1 tbsp grated Red Leicester or mild cheese

salt and pepper (optional)

peas and broccoli, to serve

2 Spoon into a shallow ovenproof dish and level the surface.

3 Roughly crush the crisps and sprinkle over the chicken. Top with the grated cheese and cook for 10 minutes, until hot and bubbly.

4 Cool slightly, then serve the pie with peas and broccoli.

1 Preheat the oven to 220°C/425°F/ Gas 7. Rinse the celery, slice thinly and place in a bowl with the corn, mayonnaise, ground coriander and a little salt and pepper, if liked. Dice the chicken, add to the bowl and mix well.

Variation
Mexican Chicken Pie
Replace the ground coriander with ground cumin and replace the crisps with about 30ml/2 tbsp crumbled plain tortilla chips.

Skinny Dippers

Serves 2

150g/5oz boneless, skinless chicken breast

25g/1oz/¼ cup grated Cheddar or mild cheese

50g/2oz/1 cup fresh breadcrumbs

15g/½oz/1 tbsp butter or margarine

115g/4oz frozen oven chips (french fries)

½ small carrot, cut into thin strips

½ small courgette (zucchini), cut into thin strips

45ml/3 tbsp tomato ketchup

1 Rinse the chicken under cold water and pat dry with kitchen paper. Cut into thin strips.

2 Mix the grated cheese and breadcrumbs on a plate. Melt the butter or margarine in a small pan or in a dish in the microwave on High (full power) for 20 seconds, then toss the chicken strips in the butter or margarine and roll in the breadcrumb mixture.

3 Arrange the chicken and chips on a foiled-lined baking sheet. Preheat the grill (broiler) and bring a pan of water to the boil.

4 Grill the chicken for 6–8 minutes and the chips 8–10 minutes, until both are well browned, turning once. When the chicken is ready, keep warm in a shallow dish while the chips finish cooking.

5 Cook the vegetables for 5 minutes in the pan of boiling water, until tender.

6 Spoon the ketchup into two ramekins or egg cups and place in the centre of two serving plates. Drain the vegetables and divide the vegetables, chicken and chips between the two plates. Allow to cool slightly before dipping into ketchup.

TIP

Keep a supply of fresh breadcrumbs in a sealed plastic bag in the freezer. There is no need to defrost, just take out as much as you need and use from frozen.

Sweet and Sour Chicken

Serves 2

50g/2oz/¼ cup long grain white rice

1 carrot, about 50g/2oz

1 courgette (zucchini), about 50g/2oz

2 skinless chicken thighs

10ml/2 tsp oil

25g/1oz/2 tbsp frozen peas

5ml/1 tsp cornflour (cornstarch)

5ml/1 tsp soy sauce

10ml/2 tsp tomato ketchup

60ml/4 tbsp orange juice

1 egg, beaten

1 Cook the rice in boiling water for 8–10 minutes, until tender.

2 Meanwhile, peel the carrot, trim the courgette and cut both into thin strips. Bone the chicken and cut into small chunks.

3 Heat 5ml/1 tsp of the oil in a frying pan, add the carrot, courgette, chicken and peas, and fry for 5 minutes, stirring occasionally.

4 Blend the cornflour with the soy sauce and then stir into the pan together with the ketchup and orange juice. Cook gently, stirring all the time, until the sauce is glossy and has thickened.

TIP
Make the meal into an occasion and serve the food in Chinese bowls with Chinese spoons – chopsticks may be a little too tricky to manage. All children love the idea of eating in a restaurant with a parent to wait on them.

5 Drain the rice thoroughly. Add the remaining oil to the rice together with the beaten egg and cook over a gentle heat, stirring until the egg has scrambled.

6 Spoon the rice and sweet and sour chicken on to serving plates and cool slightly before serving.

Ham and Tomato Scramble

Serves 2

2 slices ham

1 tomato

1 small strip yellow (bell) pepper

2 eggs

15ml/1 tbsp milk

2 slices bread

a little butter

salt

1 Finely chop the ham. Halve the tomato, scoop out and discard the seeds, then chop into small dice. Finely chop the strip of pepper.

2 Beat the eggs and milk together and season with a little salt. Toast the bread lightly.

3 Heat a small knob (pat) of butter in a pan, add the eggs, ham, tomato and pepper and cook gently, stirring all the time until cooked to taste. Cool slightly.

4 Butter the toast and cut into shapes with small fancy-shaped cookie cutters. Arrange on plates with the ham and tomato scramble.

TIP

If you don't have any special cutters, then cut the toast into tiny triangles and squares with a knife.

Ham Salad Clown

Serves 2

2 slices ham

1 cherry tomato

2 slices apple

1 slice cheese

2 currants (raisins)

2 slices hard-boiled egg

a little mustard and cress (fine curled cress)

2 long slices carrot

TIP

Have fun varying the ingredients for the clown. Use cheese slices, radishes, peaches, lettuce and red (bell) pepper to change the appearance and features.

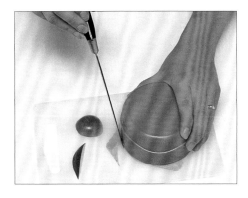

1 Cut two large rounds from the slices of ham using a cookie cutter or the top of a glass or other container as a guide. Arrange on two plates and add a halved tomato for a nose and a slice of apple for the mouth, trimming if needed.

2 With a knife, cut out small triangles or stars of cheese for eyes, place on the ham and add halved currants (raisins) for eye balls.

3 Halve the egg slices and add to the face for ears. Snip the mustard and cress for hair and use snipped pieces of carrot for a ruff.

Spanish Omelette

Serves 2

2 thin slices ham
1 strip red (bell) pepper
15ml/1 tbsp frozen peas
50g/2oz frozen oven chips (french fries)
5ml/1 tsp oil
1 egg
salt and pepper
tomato wedges, to serve

1 Chop the ham and pepper. Mix the pepper and peas. Slice the oven chips.

2 Heat the oil in a non-stick frying pan, and fry the chips for 5 minutes, stirring, until lightly browned. Add the pepper and peas and cook, stirring, for a further 2 minutes. Stir in the chopped ham.

3 Beat together the egg, 10ml/2 tsp water and a little salt and pepper, and pour into the pan, tilting it so that the egg mixture covers the base evenly.

4 Cook over a medium-low heat for 2–3 minutes, until the base of the omelette is set and browned. Loosen the edges and invert the pan on to a plate to turn out the omelette. Then slide the omelette back into the pan and cook the second side for a few more minutes, until golden.

5 Cut the omelette into wedges, arrange on two plates and cool slightly. Serve with tomato wedges.

Pasta with Ham Sauce

Serves 2

50g/2oz dried pasta shapes

50g/2oz/½ cup frozen mixed
  vegetables

30ml/2 tbsp margarine

30ml/2 tbsp plain (all-purpose) flour

150ml/¼ pint/⅔ cup milk

50g/2oz/½ cup grated Red Leicester
  or mild cheese

2 slices ham, chopped

salt and pepper

1 Cook the pasta in a pan of boiling
  water for 5 minutes. Add vegetables
and cook for 5 more minutes until
pasta is tender. Drain.

2 Melt the margarine in a
  medium-size pan and stir in the
flour. Gradually add the milk and
bring to the boil, stirring, until the
sauce is thick and smooth.

3 Stir two-thirds of the grated
  cheese into the sauce and add the
drained pasta and vegetables, the
ham and a little salt and pepper.

4 Spoon into two shallow dishes
  and sprinkle with the remaining
cheese. Cool slightly if necessary.

TIP

This recipe works equally well if
you use a 100g/3½oz can tuna,
drained, in place of the ham. You
could serve the ham with rice, if
you prefer.

Quickie Kebabs

Serves 2–3

1 tomato

3 slices ham

½ small yellow (bell) pepper

6 button (white) mushrooms

6 cocktail sausages

10ml/2 tsp tomato ketchup

10ml/2 tsp oil

canned spaghetti, to serve

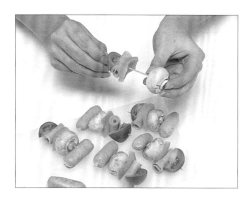

1 Preheat the grill (broiler). Cut the tomato into six wedges and cut each slice of ham into two strips. Roll up each strip. Cut the pepper into six chunks, discarding any seeds. Wipe the mushrooms.

2 Make six kebabs by threading a tomato wedge, a ham roll, a piece of pepper, a mushroom, and a sausage on to six cocktail sticks (toothpicks).

TIP
Use two rashers (strips) of rindless bacon, if preferred. Halve and roll up, and use in place of the ham.

3 Line a grill pan with foil and arrange the kebabs on top. Blend the ketchup and oil, and brush over the kebabs. Grill for 10 minutes, turning once and brushing with the juices until the vegetables are browned and the sausages are thoroughly cooked.

4 Cool slightly, then arrange on plates with canned spaghetti.

Sausage Wrappers

Serves 2

4 slices ham

10ml/2 tsp tomato relish or barbecue sauce

4 sausages

baked beans and grilled potato shapes, to serve

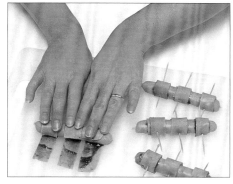

1 Spread one side of each slice of ham with relish or sauce.

2 Cut each piece of ham into three thin strips and wrap each sausage in three strips, securing them in place with cocktail sticks (toothpicks).

3 Grill (broil) for 10 minutes, turning several times until the ham is browned and crisp.

4 Cool slightly then remove the cocktail sticks and serve the sausage wrappers with baked beans and grilled potato shapes.

TIP
Use four pieces of rindless streaky (fatty) bacon instead of ham, if preferred.

Corned Beef Hash

Serves 2

1 potato, about 175g/6oz

10ml/2 tsp oil

50g/2oz green cabbage

115g/4oz corned beef

pinch of turmeric

15ml/1 tbsp tomato ketchup

hard-boiled egg slices, to garnish

1 Dice the potato and cook in a pan of boiling water for 3–4 minutes, until softened. Drain.

2 Heat the oil in a medium-size frying pan, add the diced potato and fry for 3 minutes, until golden.

3 Meanwhile, chop the cabbage and dice the corned beef.

4 Add the cabbage and turmeric to the pan with the potatoes and cook for 2 minutes. Stir in the corned beef and cook for 2 minutes.

5 Stir in the ketchup and spoon on to two plates. Cool slightly before serving. Garnish with the hard-boiled egg slices.

TIP

The hash can be garnished with tomato wedges, if liked.

Cannibal Necklaces

Serves 2

45ml/3 tbsp stuffing mix

60ml/4 tbsp boiling water

115g/4oz lean minced (ground) beef

5ml/1 tsp oil

½ carrot

1 strip red (bell) pepper

1 strip green (bell) pepper

a little tomato ketchup

1 Put the stuffing mix in a bowl and pour over the boiling water. Set aside for 5 minutes to soak.

2 Stir the meat into the stuffing mix and shape into 10 small balls with floured hands.

3 Preheat the grill (broiler). Arrange the meat balls on a piece of foil on top of the grill pan and brush lightly with a little oil. Grill (broil) for 7–8 minutes, until well browned, turning once during cooking.

4 Meanwhile, thinly slice the carrot and cut the pepper into chunks, discarding the core and seeds.

5 Arrange the meat balls around the bottom edge of two serving plates. Leave spaces in between.

TIP

If you're feeling adventurous, liven up simple meals by piping the child's initials on to the edge of the plate, the appropriate number for their age or even a short word like "hello".

6 Place carrot and pieces of red and green pepper between each meat ball and complete with a line and bow of ketchup for necklace strings, straight from the bottle, or pipe the ketchup if preferred.

Beef Burgers

Serves 2

¼ small onion

25g/1oz button (white) mushrooms

115g/4oz lean minced (ground) beef

115g/4oz frozen oven chips (french fries)

2 burger buns

10ml/2 tsp tomato ketchup

1 tomato

salt and pepper (optional)

1 Finely chop the onion, wipe and chop the mushrooms. Place the meat in a mixing bowl, add the onion and mushrooms and a little salt and pepper, if liked, and mix together thoroughly. Alternatively blend the mixture in a processor.

2 With floured hands shape two 7.5cm/3in burgers or press the mixture into a plastic burger press or upturned pastry cutter.

3 Preheat the grill (broiler). Tear off two large pieces of foil. Fold up the edges and place on a grill pan. Put the burgers on one piece and the chips on the other.

4 Cook the burgers and chips for 10 minutes, turning the food once. Remove from the grill rack and keep warm. Split the burger buns in half and toast on one side only.

5 Spread the bases of the buns with ketchup, slice the tomato and place on the buns. Top each with a burger and the second bun half. Cut in half and arrange on serving plates with the chips. Cool slightly if necessary before serving.

Four Fast Fishes

Serves 2

115g/4oz hoki or cod fillet

½ egg, beaten

60ml/4 tbsp fresh breadcrumbs

10ml/2 tsp sesame seeds

10ml/2 tsp oil

15ml/1 tbsp frozen peas

4 frozen corn kernels

1 carrot

canned spaghetti rings, to serve

1 Cut away and discard any skin from the fish and rinse. Pat dry and cut into four pieces.

2 Put the egg in a saucer and place the breadcrumbs and sesame seeds on a plate. Dip pieces of fish in egg and then in breadcrumb mixture to coat the fish.

3 Heat the oil in a frying pan, add the fish and fry for 4–5 minutes, turning once, until the fish pieces are golden brown and cooked.

4 Meanwhile cook the peas and corn in a pan of boiling water for 5 minutes. Cut the carrot into long thin slices and then cut out fin and tail shapes and tiny triangles for mouths.

5 Arrange the pieces of fish on two plates with the carrot decorations, corn for eyes and peas for bubbles. Serve with warmed canned spaghetti rings.

TIP

You can freeze the uncooked breaded portions to provide a quick meal at a later date when you are pushed for time. Freeze them on a tray and then wrap them well to prevent the odour tainting other food in the freezer.

Tuna Risotto

Serves 2

5ml/1 tsp oil

¼ onion, finely chopped

50g/2oz long grain white rice

50g/2oz frozen mixed vegetables

1 small garlic clove, crushed

10ml/2 tsp tomato ketchup

100g/3½oz can tuna fish in water

salt and pepper (optional)

1 Heat the oil in a small pan and fry the chopped onion for about 3 minutes, until softened.

2 Add the rice, mixed vegetables, garlic, tomato ketchup and 250ml/8fl oz/1 cup water and a little salt and pepper, if liked.

TIP

If liked use cold leftover cooked chicken, lamb or beef in place of the tuna.

3 Bring to the boil and simmer uncovered for 10 minutes. Drain the tuna and add to the rice mixture, stirring to mix. Cook for 3–4 minutes, stirring occasionally, until the water has been absorbed by the rice and the rice is tender.

4 Spoon on to plates and cool slightly before serving.

Fish Finger Log Cabins

Serves 2

4 frozen fish fingers (breaded fish sticks)

25g/1oz green cabbage

8 mangetouts (snow peas)

2 frozen peas

1 strip green (bell) pepper

1 strip red (bell) pepper

1 Grill (broil) the fish fingers for 10 minutes, turning once until golden. Meanwhile, finely shred the cabbage and cook in boiling water for 3 minutes. Add the mangetouts and peas and cook for a further 2 minutes. Drain well.

2 Arrange two fish fingers side by side on each plate. Trim the mangetouts and use them to make a roof, slightly overlapping the edges of the fish fingers.

VARIATION
Sausage Log Cabin
Use four grilled (broiled) cocktail chipolata sausages for each cabin. Make the roof from green beans and use shredded spinach for the grass.

3 Cut four windows from the green pepper and two doors from the red pepper and add to the log cabins, using peas as door handles. Arrange the shredded cabbage to look like grass.

TOAST TOPPERS

ALL CHILDREN, EVEN THE FUSSIEST OF EATERS, LOVE BREAD AND TOAST, AND THERE IS NO QUICKER CONVENIENCE FOOD. RING THE CHANGES WITH THESE SUPER-SPEEDY SNACKS THAT WILL MAKE MEAL-TIMES FUN.

Shape Sorters

Serves 2

4 slices bread

butter or margarine, for spreading

30ml/2 tbsp smooth peanut butter

50g/2oz/½ cup grated Cheddar or mild cheese

4 cherry tomatoes

3 slices cucumber

VARIATION
Pizza Shape Sorters
Spread the shapes with tomato ketchup. Chop a tomato finely, and sprinkle over the shapes, then add some grated mild cheese. Grill (broil) until bubbly and golden.

1 Toast the bread lightly on both sides and remove crusts. Stamp out shapes using square, star, triangle and round cutters.

2 Spread the shapes with butter or margarine and then peanut butter. Place the shapes on a baking sheet and sprinkle with cheese.

3 Grill (broil) until the cheese is bubbly. Cool slightly, arrange on a plate and serve with tomato wedges and quartered cucumber slices.

Happy Families

Serves 2

3 slices bread

butter or margarine, for spreading

3 slices processed cheese

2 slices ham

a little mustard and cress (fine curled cress)

1 strip red (bell) pepper

½ carrot

small pieces of cucumber

1 Stamp out shapes of men and women from the bread, using small cutters. Spread with a little butter or margarine.

2 Stamp out cheese dresses using the woman cutter and trimming off the head. Press on to three of the bodies. Cut out cheese jumpers and ham trousers and braces. Add to the male shapes.

3 Snip off the leaves from mustard and cress and use for eyes. Cut tiny red pepper mouths and make necklaces and bow ties from the carrot and cucumber, using flower cutters. Arrange on plates.

French Toast Butterflies

Serves 2

4 small broccoli florets
8 peas
1 small carrot
1 slice Red Leicester or mild cheese
2 slices ham
2 slices bread
1 egg
10ml/2 tsp milk
5ml/1 tsp vegetable oil
a little tomato ketchup

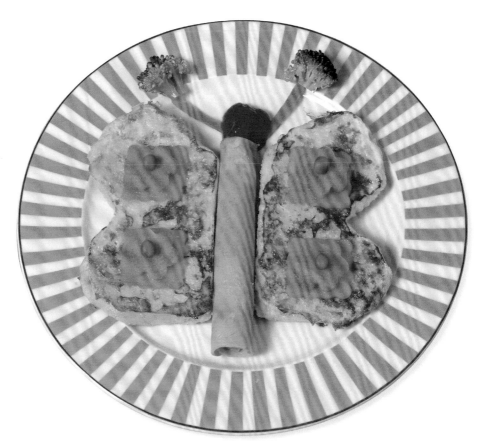

1 Cook the broccoli florets and the peas in a pan of boiling water for 5 minutes. Drain well.

2 For each butterfly, cut four thin slices of carrot and cut into flower shapes with a petits four cutter. Cut out four small squares from the cheese.

3 Cut four thin strips from the rest of the carrot for antennae. Roll up each piece of ham and arrange in the middle of two serving plates, to make the two butterfly bodies.

4 Cut butterfly wings from the bread, using a small knife.

TIP
Vary the ingredients for the butterfly decorations. Make a body from a grilled sausage if preferred.

5 Beat together the egg and milk and dip the bread in to coat both sides thoroughly. Heat the oil in a medium-size frying pan and fry the bread until golden on both sides.

6 Assemble the butterfly, using the French toast for the wings and decorating with the carrot, cheese, broccoli and peas. Use a blob of ketchup for the head.

Tuna Flowers

Serves 2–3

6 thin slices bread

25g/1oz butter, plus extra if
  necessary

10ml/2 tsp plain (all-purpose) flour

75ml/5 tbsp milk

60ml/4 tbsp grated Red Leicester or
  mild cheese

100g/3½oz can tuna fish, drained

50g/2oz/4 tbsp frozen mixed
  vegetables, defrosted

½ carrot

6 slices cucumber, halved

a little mustard and cress (fine curled
  cress)

salt and pepper (optional)

1 Preheat the oven to 200°C/
400°F/Gas 6. Cut out six flower
shapes from the bread, using a 9cm/
3½in scalloped cookie cutter. Flatten
each piece slightly with a rolling pin.

4 Stir the flour into the remaining
butter (you should have about
10ml/2 tsp left). Gradually stir in the
milk and bring to the boil, stirring
until the sauce is thick and smooth.

5 Stir in 30ml/3 tbsp of the cheese,
the tuna, the mixed vegetables
and a little salt and pepper, if liked.

6 Heat through and then spoon
into the baked bread cups and
sprinkle with remaining cheese.

7 Arrange the tuna cups on
serving plates. Cut the carrot
into thin strips for flower stems and
add to the plate, with halved
cucumber slices for leaves and
mustard and cress for grass.

2 Melt the butter in a pan or
microwave. Brush a little over
one side of each piece of bread and
then press the bread, buttered side
downwards, into sections of a patty tin
(muffin pan). Brush the second side of
the bread with a little more butter.

3 Bake in the oven for about 10–
12 minutes, until crisp and
golden around the edges.

Noughts and Crosses

Serves 2

8 green beans

¼ red (bell) pepper

6 slices snack dried sausage

2 slices bread

butter or margarine, for spreading

115g/4oz Cheddar or mild cheese

TIP
To vary the topping, use thin strips of carrot or ham for the grid, sliced sausage, frankfurter or carrot for the noughts (zeros), carrot, green (bell) pepper or cucumber for the crosses.

1 Trim the beans, thinly slice the pepper, discarding any seeds, and thinly slice the sausage.

2 Cook the beans in boiling water for 5 minutes. Toast the bread lightly on both sides and spread with butter or margarine. Thinly slice the cheese and place on the toast.

3 Drain the beans and arrange four on each piece of toast to form a grid. Add crosses made from pepper strips and noughts from pieces of the sausage.

4 Grill (broil) the toasts until the cheese is bubbly. Arrange on plates and cool slightly before serving.

Cheese Strips on Toast

Serves 2

2 slices bread

butter or margarine, for spreading

50g/2oz Cheddar or mild yellow cheese

50g/2oz red Leicester or mild red cheese

2 cherry tomatoes, to serve

1 Toast the bread lightly on both sides, then spread each slice with butter or margarine.

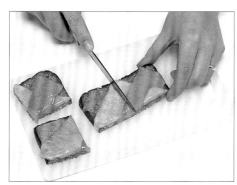

TIP
If your child likes ketchup or peanut butter, add a thin scraping underneath the cheese slices for a surprise flavour.

2 Thinly slice the cheese and then cut into strips about 2.5cm/1in wide. Arrange alternate coloured cheese strips over the toast and grill (broil) the toasts until bubbly.

3 Cool slightly, then cut into squares, arrange on plates and serve with cherry tomato wedges.

Speedy Sausage Rolls

Makes 18

8 slices multigrain white bread

225g/8oz cocktail sausages

40g/1½oz/3 tbsp butter or
  margarine

carrot and cucumber sticks, to serve

1 Preheat the oven to 190°C/
375°F/Gas 5. Trim the crusts off
the bread and cut into slices a little
smaller than the sausages.

2 Wrap each piece of bread around
a sausage and secure with a
halved cocktail stick (toothpick). Place
the sausage rolls on a baking sheet.

3 Melt the butter or margarine in a
small pan or in the microwave and
brush over the prepared sausage rolls.

4 Bake in the oven for 15 minutes,
until browned. Cool slightly
and remove the cocktail sticks.
Arrange on a plate and serve with
carrot and cucumber sticks.

TIP
Spread a little tomato relish or
ketchup, or a little mild mustard
over the bread before wrapping it
around the sausages, to give a
sharper flavour. If the bread is
thickly cut, flatten it slightly with a
rolling pin, before wrapping around
the sausages.

Pizza Clock

Serves 3–4

20cm/8in ready-made pizza base

45ml/3 tbsp tomato ketchup or pizza sauce

2 tomatoes

75g/3oz/¾ cup grated mild cheese

pinch of dried marjoram

1 green (bell) pepper

1 large carrot

1 thick slice ham

1 Preheat oven to 220°C/425°F/ Gas 7. Place the pizza base on a baking sheet and spread with ketchup or pizza sauce. Chop the tomatoes and scatter over the pizza with the cheese and marjoram.

2 Place directly on an oven shelf and bake for 12 minutes, until the cheese is bubbly. (Place a baking tray on the shelf below the pizza to catch any drips of cheese.)

3 Meanwhile halve the pepper, cut away the core and seeds and stamp out the numbers 3, 6, 9 and 12 with small number cutters. Peel and thinly cut the carrot lengthways and stamp out the numbers 1, 2, 4, 5, 7, 8, 10 and 11. Arrange on the pizza to form a clock face.

4 Cut out a carrot circle. Cut two clock hands, each about 7.5cm/ 3in long from the ham. Arrange on the pizza with the circle of carrot.

5 Place the pizza clock on to a serving plate and arrange the numbers around the edge. Cool the pizza clock slightly before cutting into wedges and serving.

TIP

If preferred, make a smaller version of this using half a toasted muffin. Top as above and grill (broil) until the cheese melts. Add ham hands and small pieces of carrot to mark the numbers.

Spotted Sandwiches

Serves 2

1 hard-boiled egg

30ml/2 tbsp mayonnaise

2 slices white bread

2 slices brown bread

a little mustard and cress (fine curled cress)

½ small carrot

1 Peel and finely chop the egg, place in a small bowl and blend well with the mayonnaise.

2 Stamp out giraffe shapes from the brown and white bread, using an animal cookie cutter.

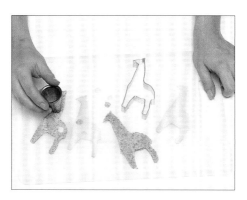

3 Cut tiny rounds from each shape, using the end of a metal piping tube, and then replace the rounds with opposite-coloured bread circles.

4 Spread the egg and mayonnaise over half of the shapes and top with the remaining shapes. Arrange on plates with snipped mustard and cress for grass and shaped carrot slices for flowers.

Sandwich Snails

Serves 2

1 strip red (bell) pepper

small piece cucumber

15ml/1 tbsp frozen corn, defrosted

25g/1oz/¼ cup grated Cheddar or mild cheese

15ml/1 tbsp mayonnaise

1 slice bread

2 cooked sausages

a little shredded lettuce

1 Cut away any seeds from the pepper and cut out four small squares for the snails' eyes. Cut four strips of cucumber for their antennae. Finely chop the remaining pepper and cucumber and mix with the corn, cheese and mayonnaise. Place in a bowl.

2 Trim the crusts off the bread, cut in half and overlap two short edges together to make a long strip. Flatten slightly with a rolling pin so that the bread bonds together.

VARIATION
For pasta snails, use large shell pasta instead of the bread, and stuff with the cheese mixture.

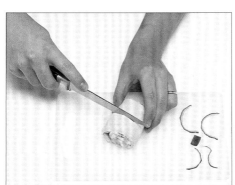

3 Spread the bread with the cheese mixture and roll up tightly. Squeeze together, then cut in half crossways to make two rounds.

4 Arrange each slice, cut side uppermost, on two serving plates. Arrange the sausages as bodies, and use the cucumber strips for antennae and the red pepper squares for the eyes. Arrange the shredded lettuce as grass.

Easy Desserts

With a young family to feed, desserts need to be quick, light and taste good without the kids realizing that they're healthy too! Remember to keep sugar to a minimum.

Fruit Fondue

Serves 2

150g/5oz tub ready-to-serve low-fat custard

25g/1oz milk chocolate

1 eating apple

1 banana

1 satsuma or clementine

a few strawberries or seedless grapes

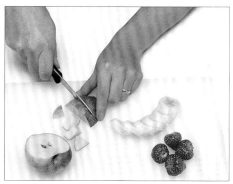

1 Pour the custard into a pan, add the chocolate and heat, stirring all the time until the chocolate has melted. Cool slightly.

2 Quarter the apple, core and cut into bitesize pieces, slice the banana and break the satsuma or clementine into segments. Hull the strawberries and wash the grapes.

3 Arrange the fruit on two small plates, pour the custard into two small dishes and place on the plates. The fruit can be dipped into the custard, using either a fork or fingers.

TIP
Add the chocolate to a tub of custard and microwave on Full Power (100%) for 1½ minutes, or until the chocolate has melted. Stir and spoon into dishes. Cool slightly.

Strawberry Ice Cream

Makes 900ml/1½ pints/3¾ cups

300ml/½pint/1¼ cups double (heavy) cream

425g/15oz can custard

450g/1lb strawberries

teddy bear wafers, to decorate

strawberries, to decorate

1 Whip the cream until softly peaking, then fold in the custard.

2 Hull the strawberries and then rinse and pat dry. Process to make a smooth purée, then press through a sieve (strainer) into the cream and custard. Fold together.

3 Pour the mixture into a plastic tub and freeze the ice cream for 6-7 hours, until half frozen.

4 Beat the ice cream with a fork or process in a food blender until smooth, then return the tub to the freezer and freeze until solid.

5 Remove the ice cream from the freezer 10 minutes before serving so that it can soften slightly. Scoop into serving bowls and decorate each with teddy bear wafers and extra fruit, such as strawberries.

VARIATIONS
Strawberry Ripple Ice Cream
Purée and sieve (strain) an extra 250g/9oz strawberries and sweeten with 30ml/2 tbsp icing (confectioners') sugar. Swirl this into the half-frozen ice cream at Step 4 and then freeze until solid.

Apricot and Chocolate Chip Ice Cream
Whisk 300ml/½ pint/1¼ cups double (heavy) cream, and fold in 425g/15oz can custard. Drain and purée the contents of a 425g/15oz can apricot slices in natural juice and stir into the cream with the finely grated rind of 1 orange. Pour into a plastic tub, freeze until mushy and then beat well. Stir in 100g/3½oz packet chocolate dots and freeze again until solid. Scoop into serving dishes and decorate the ice cream with orange segments and wafers, if liked.

Raspberry Sorbet

Makes: 900ml/1½ pints/3¾ cups

10ml/2 tsp powdered gelatine

600ml/1 pint/2½ cups water

225g/8oz/1¼ cups caster (superfine) sugar

675g/1½lb raspberries, hulled

grated rind and juice of ½ lemon

1 Put 30ml/2 tbsp water in a cup, sprinkle the gelatine over and set aside for a few minutes to soak.

2 Place the water and sugar in a pan and heat, stirring occasionally, until the sugar has completely dissolved.

3 Bring to the boil and boil rapidly for 3 minutes. Remove from the heat, add the gelatine mixture to the syrup and stir until completely dissolved. Leave to cool.

4 Liquidize or process the raspberries to a smooth purée, then press through a sieve (strainer) into the syrup. Stir in the lemon rind and juice.

5 Pour into a plastic tub and freeze for 6–7 hours, or until the mixture is half frozen.

6 Beat the sorbet with a fork or transfer to a food processor and process until smooth. Return to the freezer and freeze until solid.

7 Remove the sorbet from the freezer 10 minutes before serving to soften slightly, then scoop into dishes with a melon baller or small teaspoon.

VARIATION
Summer Fruit Sorbet
Follow the recipe up to Step 3. Put a 500g/1¼lb pack of frozen summer fruits into a second pan. Add 60ml/ 4 tbsp water, cover and cook for 5 minutes until soft, then purée and sieve (strain), add to the syrup and continue as above.

Yogurt Lollies

Makes 6

150g/5oz tub strawberry yogurt

150ml/¼ pint/⅔ cup milk

10ml/2 tsp strawberry milkshake powder

1 Mix the yogurt, milk and milkshake powder together.

2 Pour the mixture into six small lolly (popsicle) plastic moulds. Add the handles and freeze overnight.

TIP

Store lollies (popsicles) for up to a week in the freezer. Make sure they are tightly covered, as they can pick up other flavours.

3 Dip the moulds into hot water, count to 15, then flex handles and remove. Serve at once.

Jolly Jellies

Serves 4

150g/5oz packet strawberry jelly (flavoured gelatine)

2 ripe plums

175g/6oz fromage frais or Greek (US strained plain) yogurt

4 dolly mixtures (round candies)

10ml/2 tsp sugar or chocolate strands

1 Cut the jelly into pieces. Place in a bowl and pour over 150ml/ ¼ pint/⅔ cup boiling water. Stir until dissolved, then set aside to cool.

2 Halve the plums, cut away the stones (pits) and reserve four thin slices. Chop the remaining fruit and divide among four small dishes.

TIP

If the fussy eater doesn't like different textures, finely chop or purée the plums before adding to the jelly (flavoured gelatine) so the child doesn't know it's not just jelly!

3 Stir the fromage frais or yogurt into the jelly and pour into the dishes. Chill in the refrigerator until set.

4 Decorate with sliced plums for mouths, halved dolly mixtures for the eyes and sugar or chocolate sugar strands for hair.

Pancakes

Serves 2–3

50g/2oz/⅓ cup plain (all-purpose) flour

1 egg

150ml/¼ pint/⅔ cup milk

15ml/1 tbsp vegetable oil

For the filling

1 banana

1 orange

2–3 scoops ice cream

1 Sift the flour into a bowl, add the egg and gradually whisk in the milk to form a smooth batter. Whisk in 5ml/1 tsp of the oil.

2 To make the filling, slice the banana thinly or in chunks. Cut the peel away from the orange with a serrated knife, then cut the orange into segments.

3 Heat a little of the remaining oil in a medium-size non-stick pan, pour off any excess oil and add 30ml/2 tbsp of the batter. Tilt the pan to evenly coat it and cook for a couple of minutes, until the pancake is set and the underside is golden.

4 Loosen the edges with a knife, then toss the pancake or turn with a knife. Brown the other side and then slide out on to a plate. Fold in four and keep warm.

5 Cook the rest of the batter in the same way until you have made 6 pancakes. Place two on each plate.

6 Spoon a little fruit into each pancake and arrange on serving plates. Top with the remaining fruit and a scoop of ice cream, and pour over a little maple syrup. Serve at once.

Traffic Light Sundaes

Serves 6

½ packet lime jelly (flavoured gelatine)

½ packet orange jelly

½ packet strawberry jelly

2 kiwi fruits

275g/10oz can mandarin oranges

6 scoops vanilla ice cream, to serve

12 strawberries to decorate

4 Add a little kiwi fruit and continue making layers using the orange jelly and mandarins and topping with the strawberry jelly.

5 Add half the strawberries, top with a scoop of ice cream and decorate with the remaining strawberries. Serve immediately.

1 Make up each jelly in a separate bowl with boiling water according to the instructions on the packet. Cool, then transfer to the refrigerator and allow to set.

2 Peel and slice the kiwi fruits, hull and rinse the strawberries and cut in half. Drain the mandarins.

3 Chop all of the jellies and divide the lime jelly equally among six sundae glasses.

TIP

This is a great recipe for a party – simple but ever popular. For smaller numbers of children, halve the recipe to make three. For tiny children, make up half-size sundaes in plastic cups.

Cheat's Trifle

Serves 2

2 slices Swiss roll (jelly roll)

20ml/4 tsp orange juice

1 mandarin orange

50g/2oz strawberries

150g/5oz tub ready-to-serve custard

10ml/2 tsp Greek (US strained plain) yogurt

2 sugar flowers, to decorate

TIP
Use 150ml/¼ pint/⅔ cup leftover custard if you have it or make custard with custard powder and 150ml/¼ pint/⅔ cup milk.

1 Put a slice of Swiss roll in the base of two ramekin dishes and spoon the orange juice over the top. Peel the mandarin orange and divide the segments between the dishes.

2 Hull, rinse and chop the strawberries. Place in dishes.

3 Spoon the custard over the strawberries, top with yogurt and decorate with sugar flowers.

Baked Bananas

Serves 2

2 medium bananas

2 small scoops ice cream

1 Preheat the oven to 180°C/ 350°F/Gas 4. Separate the unpeeled bananas and put on a baking sheet. Cook for 10 minutes, until the skins have blackened and the bananas feel quite soft.

2 Hold the banana in a dish towel, make a slit along the length of the banana and peel off the skin. Peel the second banana.

3 Slice and arrange each as a ring on a plate. Place a scoop of ice cream in the centre of each plate.

TIP
For an adult version, slit the banana and spoon in a teaspoon or two of coffee cream liqueur, eat out of the skin with a teaspoon.

QUICK CAKES AND BAKES THE KIDS CAN MAKE

Cooking is fun, and the earlier you learn, the more fun it is. Even the faddiest eater can be an enthusiastic cook, and helping to decide what to cook for a meal can make a child more willing to sit down with the family and hand round their home-made goodies. Learning to weigh out ingredients, and to mix, spread and spoon out, all helps with co-ordination and encourages a basic interest in and love of food.

Getting ready
- Find a large apron or cover the child's clothes with an old adult-size shirt with the sleeves cut down.
- Always wash the child's hands before you start to cook.

- Choose a sturdy chair for your child to stand on next to the work surface or table. Alternatively, put a large cloth on the floor, set scales, bowls, ingredients etc out, and prepare food sitting down.

- Make it clear to your child that only the adult opens the oven door and touches pans on the stove.
- Keep knives and scissors out of the way; provide blunt, round-ended scissors if required.

Orange and Apple Rockies

Makes 24

oil, for greasing
115g/4oz/½ cup margarine
225g/8oz/2 cups self-raising (self-rising) flour
1 large eating apple
50g/2oz ready-to-eat dried apricots
50g/2oz sultanas (golden raisins)
grated rind of 1 small orange
75g/3oz/⅓ cup demerara (raw) sugar
1 egg
15ml/1 tbsp milk
apple slices, to serve

1 Preheat the oven to 190°C/375°F/ Gas 5 and brush two baking sheets with a little oil. Rub the margarine into the flour with your fingertips until the mixture resembles fine breadcrumbs.

2 Peel, core and finely chop the apple, chop the apricots and stir into the flour mixture with the sultanas and orange rind. Reserve 30ml/2 tbsp of the sugar and stir the rest into the mixture.

3 Beat the egg and milk, add to the flour mixture and mix until just beginning to bind together.

4 Drop spoonfuls, well spaced apart, on to the baking sheet. Sprinkle with the reserved sugar and bake in the oven for 12–15 minutes. Transfer to a serving plate and serve warm or cold with apple slices.

TIP
Freeze any left-over rockies in a plastic bag for up to three months.

Date Crunch

Makes 24 pieces

225g/8oz packet digestive biscuits (graham crackers)

75g/3oz stoned (pitted) dates

75g/3oz/⅓ cup butter

30ml/2 tbsp golden (light corn) syrup

75g/3oz sultanas (golden raisins)

150g/5oz milk or dark (bittersweet) chocolate

1 Line an 18cm/7in shallow baking tin (pan) with foil. Put the biscuits in a plastic bag and crush roughly with a rolling pin. Finely chop the dates.

2 Gently heat the butter and syrup in a small pan until the butter has melted.

TIP

For an alternative topping, drizzle 75g/3oz melted white and 75g/3oz melted dark (bittersweet) chocolate over the biscuit, to make random squiggly lines. Chill until set.

3 Stir in the crushed biscuits, the dates and sultanas and mix well. Spoon into the tin, press flat with the back of a spoon and chill for 1 hour.

4 Break the chocolate into a bowl, melt over hot water, and then spoon over the biscuit mixture, spreading evenly with a palette knife. Chill until set.

5 Lift the foil out of the tin and peel away. Cut the biscuit into 24 pieces and arrange on a plate.

Chocolate Dominoes

Makes 16

oil, for greasing

175g/6oz/¾ cup soft margarine

175g/6oz/⅞ cup caster (superfine) sugar

150g/5oz/⅔ cup self-raising (self-rising) flour

25g/1oz cocoa powder (unsweetened)

3 eggs

For the Topping

175g/6oz/¾ cup butter, softened

25g/1oz cocoa powder (unsweetened)

300g/11oz/3 cups icing (confectioners') sugar

a few liquorice strips and 115g/4oz packet M & M's, for decoration

1 Preheat the oven to 180°C/350°F/ Gas 4. Brush an 18 × 28cm/7 × 11in baking tin (pan) with a little oil and line with baking parchment.

2 Put all the cake ingredients in a bowl and beat until smooth.

3 Spoon into the tin and level the surface with a palette knife.

4 Bake in the oven for 30 minutes, or until the cake springs back when pressed with the fingertips.

5 Cool in the tin for 5 minutes, then loosen the edges with a knife and turn out on to a wire rack. Peel off the paper and allow the cake to cool.

6 Turn the cake on to a chopping board and cut into 16 bars.

7 To make the topping, place the butter in a bowl, sift in the cocoa and icing sugar and beat until smooth. Spread the topping evenly over the cakes with a palette knife.

8 Add a strip of liquorice to each cake, decorate with M & M's for domino dots and arrange the cakes on a serving plate.

VARIATION
Traffic Light Cakes
Makes 16
To make Traffic Light Cakes omit the cocoa and add an extra 25g/1oz/3 tbsp flour. Omit the cocoa from the icing and add an extra 25g/1oz/3 tbsp icing (confectioners') sugar and flavour with 2.5ml/½ tsp vanilla essence (extract). Spread over the cakes and decorate with eight halved red, yellow and green glacé (candied) cherries to look like traffic lights.

Marshmallow Krispie Cakes

Makes 45

oil, for greasing

250g/9oz bag toffees

50g/2oz/4 tbsp butter

45ml/3 tbsp milk

115g/4oz marshmallows

175g/6oz Rice Krispies

1 Lightly brush a 20 × 33cm/8 × 13in roasting pan with a little oil. Put the toffees, butter and milk in a pan and heat gently, stirring until the toffees have melted.

2 Add the marshmallows and Rice Krispies and stir until well mixed and the marshmallows have melted.

3 Spoon into the pan, level the surface and leave to set. Cut into squares, put into paper cases and serve.

Mini-muffins

Makes 24

200g/7oz/1½ cups plain (all-purpose) flour

10ml/2 tsp baking powder

50g/2oz/¼ cup soft light brown sugar

150ml/¼ pint/⅔ cup milk

1 egg, beaten

50g/2oz/4 tbsp butter or margarine, melted

50g/2oz glacé (candied) cherries

50g/2oz ready-to-eat dried apricots

2.5ml/½ tsp vanilla essence (extract)

1 Preheat the oven to 220°C/ 425°F/Gas 7 and place 24 petits fours cases in two mini patty tins (muffin pans).

2 Place the flour, baking powder and sugar in a bowl and add the milk, egg and melted butter or margarine. Stir thoroughly until the mixture is smooth.

3 Chop the cherries and apricots and stir into the muffin mixture with the vanilla essence.

4 Spoon the muffin mixture into the paper cases so they are about three-quarters full.

5 Cook for 10–12 minutes, until well risen and browned. If you have just one tin cook in two batches.

TIP
For older children, spoon the mixture into 12 medium-size muffin cases. Muffins are best served warm from the oven. If they aren't eaten immediately, they can be frozen for up to three months.

VARIATIONS
Chocolate Chip Muffins
Substitute 25g/1oz unsweetened cocoa powder for 25g/1oz/2 tbsp flour. Omit the cherries, apricots and vanilla and substitute 50g/2oz white and 50g/2oz plain (semisweet) chocolate dots.

Orange and Banana Muffins
Substitute 2 small mashed bananas for 60ml/2fl oz/¼ cup milk. Omit the cherries, apricot and vanilla, and add 15ml/1 tbsp grated orange rind.

Cup Cake Faces

Makes 12

115g/4oz/⅔ cup margarine

115g/4oz/⅔ cup caster (superfine) sugar

115g/4oz/1 cup self-raising (self-rising) flour

2 eggs

For the Topping

50g/2oz/¼ cup butter

115g/4oz/1 cup icing (confectioners') sugar

pink food colouring

115g/4oz packet M & M's

2 red liquorice bootlaces

12 dolly mixtures

75g/3oz plain (semisweet) chocolate

1 Preheat the oven to 180°C/350°F/ Gas 4. Place 12 paper cake cases in the sections of a patty tin (muffin pan). Put all the cake ingredients into a bowl and beat until smooth.

2 Divide the cake mixture among the cases and cook for 12–15 minutes, until well risen and the cakes spring back when pressed with a fingertip. Leave to cool.

3 Meanwhile, make the topping: beat the butter in a bowl, sift in the icing sugar and beat the mixture until smooth. Stir in a little pink food colouring.

4 Spread the icing over the cakes. Add M & M eyes, short pieces of liquorice for mouths and a dolly mixture nose.

5 Break the chocolate into pieces, melt in a bowl over a pan of gently simmering water and then spoon into a baking parchment piping (pastry) bag. Snip off the tip and pipe hair, eye balls, glasses and moustaches on to the cakes.

6 Carefully arrange in a single layer on a serving plate and allow the icing to set before serving.

VARIATION
Alphabet Cakes
Make up a half quantity of cake mixture as above and spoon into 24 mini muffin or petits fours cases. Put into sections of a patty tin (muffin pan) or petits fours tin (pan), or arrange on a baking sheet close together, and cook for 8–10 minutes, then cool. Blend 225g/8oz/2 cups sifted icing (confectioners') sugar with 30ml/2tbsp water until smooth. Add a little water if necessary, to make a thick spoonable icing. Spoon 30ml/2 tbsp into a piping (pastry) bag fitted with a small nozzle. Spoon half the remaining icing into a separate bowl and colour pink. Colour the remaining icing blue. Spoon the icing over the cakes, smooth the surface and pipe on letters of the alphabet. Leave to set.

Gingerbread People

Makes 24

oil, for greasing

225g/8oz/2 cups plain (all-purpose) flour

5ml/1 tsp ground ginger

1.5ml/¼ tsp ground cinnamon

7.5ml/1½ tsp bicarbonate of soda (baking soda)

50g/2oz/4 tbsp margarine

115g/4oz/⅔ cup soft light brown sugar

45ml/3 tbsp golden (light corn) syrup

30ml/2 tbsp milk

75g/3oz dark (bittersweet) chocolate

2 packets M & M's

1 Brush two baking sheets with a little oil. Sift the flour, spices and bicarbonate of soda into a bowl.

2 Place the margarine, sugar and syrup in a pan and heat until the margarine has melted.

3 Remove from heat and stir in the flour mixture and milk. Mix to a firm dough, chill for 30 minutes.

TIP
Chocolate decorations soften biscuits (cookies), so eat on the day or decorate as many biscuits as you will eat and store the rest in an air-tight container for up to four days.

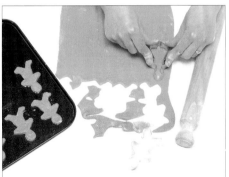

4 Preheat the oven to 160°C/ 325°F/Gas 3. Knead the dough lightly and roll out on a floured surface. Cut out gingerbread men and women with 9cm/3½in cutters. Place on the baking sheets, re roll the trimmings, stamp out nine gingerbread people and continue until all the dough is used.

5 Cook for 10 minutes, until golden, and then set aside to cool and harden a little on the baking sheets. Loosen while still warm.

6 Break the chocolate into a bowl and melt over hot water, then spoon a little chocolate over the gingerbread men for trousers. Place on the baking sheets to set.

7 Spoon the remaining chocolate into a piping (pastry) bag fitted with a small nozzle and pipe faces on the gingerbread people and some swirls for petticoats on the women. Pipe two dots on all the people for buttons and stick on M & M's. Leave to set before serving.

Bread Animals

Makes 15

| oil, for greasing |
| 2 × 280g/10oz packets white bread mix |
| a few currants (raisins) |
| ½ small red (bell) pepper |
| 1 small carrot |
| 1 egg |

1 Brush two large baking sheets with a little oil. Put the bread mixes in a large bowl and make up as directed on the packet, with warm water.

2 Knead on a lightly floured surface for 5 minutes, until the dough is smooth and elastic. Return the dough to the bowl, cover with oiled clear film (plastic wrap) and leave in a warm place for ¾–1 hour, until it has doubled in size.

3 Preheat the oven to 220°C/ 425°F/Gas 7. Knead the dough again for 5 minutes and then divide into five pieces.

4 To make snakes, take one piece of dough, cut into three and shape each into a 15cm/6in snake, making a slit in one end for the mouth. Twist the snakes on the baking sheet. Insert two currants for eyes. Cut out a thin strip of pepper, cutting a triangle at one end for the forked tongue.

5 For hedgehogs, take another piece of dough and cut into three. Shape each into an oval about 6cm/2½in long. Place on the baking sheet and add currant eyes and a red pepper nose. Snip the dough with scissors to make the prickly spines.

6 For the mice, take a third piece of dough and cut into four pieces. Shape three pieces into ovals, each about 6cm/2½in long and place on the baking sheet. Shape tiny rounds of dough for ears and wiggly tails from the fourth piece of dough. Press on to the mice bodies and use the currants for eyes.

7 Cut small strips of carrot and use for whiskers.

TIP
Give a portion of the prepared dough to your children, with some chopped dried fruits, and allow them to create their very own bread animals.

8 For the crocodiles, cut another piece of dough into three. Take a small piece off each and reserve. Shape the large pieces into 10cm/4in long sausages. Make slits for the mouths and wedge open with crumpled foil. Add currant eyes. Shape the spare dough into feet and press into position. Make criss-cross cuts on the backs.

9 For rabbits, take the final piece of dough and cut into three. Take a small piece off each for tails. Roll the remaining pieces of dough into thick sausages 18cm/7in long. Loop the dough and twist twice to form the body and head of rabbit. Use the rest for tails.

10 Cover the shapes with oiled clear film and leave in a warm place for 10–15 minutes. Brush with beaten egg and cook for 10–12 minutes, until golden.

11 Serve warm or cold, split and filled with ham or cheese.

Cheese Shapes

Makes 15

oil, for greasing

350g/12oz/3 cups self-raising (self-rising) flour

pinch of salt

115g/4oz/½ cup margarine

115g/4oz Cheddar or mild cheese

2 eggs, beaten

60ml/4 tbsp milk

10ml/2 tsp sesame seeds

10ml/2 tsp poppy seeds

1 Preheat the oven to 220°C/ 425°F/Gas 7.

2 Place the flour and salt in a bowl, add the margarine and rub in with your fingertips, or use an electric mixer, until the mixture resembles fine breadcrumbs.

3 Grate the cheese, reserve 30ml/ 2 tbsp and stir the rest into the flour. Add three-quarters of the beaten eggs and milk to the flour and mix to a soft dough.

4 Knead the dough lightly and roll out thickly on a surface that has been dusted with flour.

5 Stamp out numbers with 7cm/3in cutters and arrange well spaced apart on two baking sheets. Re-roll trimmings and stamp out more shapes to use up the pastry.

6 Brush the tops of the numbers with the reserved egg. Sprinkle five of the numbers with sesame seeds, five with poppy seeds and the remainder with grated cheese.

7 Cook for 12–15 minutes, until well risen and browned. Cool slightly, then arrange the shapes on a plate and serve warm.

Marmite and Cheese Whirls

Makes 16

oil, for greasing

250g/9oz frozen puff pastry, defrosted

flour, for dusting

2.5ml/½ tsp Marmite

1 egg, beaten

50g/2oz Red Leicester, Cheddar or mild cheese, grated

carrot and cucumber sticks, to serve

1 Preheat the oven to 220°C/ 425°F/Gas 7 and brush a large baking sheet with a little oil.

2 Roll out the pastry on a floured surface to a large rectangle, about 35 × 25cm/14 × 10in.

3 Spread the pastry with Marmite, leaving a 1 cm/½in border. Brush the edges of the pastry with egg and sprinkle the cheese to cover the Marmite.

TIP
Omit the Marmite and use peanut butter if preferred. If the shapes become a little squashed when sliced, reform into rounds by opening out the layers with the end of a knife.

4 Roll the pastry up quite tightly like a Swiss roll (jelly roll), starting from a longer edge. Brush the outside of the pastry with beaten egg.

5 Cut the roll into thick slices and place on the baking sheet.

6 Cook for 12–15 minutes until the pastry is well risen and golden. Arrange on a serving plate and serve warm or cold with carrot and cucumber sticks.

FAMILY MEALS

Eating together as a family takes on a new dimension as your family grows and there's a baby, fussy toddler and parents to feed together. Rather than attempting to prepare three different meals or to make one very simple meal you know the children will like, opt instead to cook three meals from one basic

set of ingredients: a simple baby dinner, an eye-catching meal for even the fussiest of toddlers and a spicy dinner for the grown-ups.

The recipes are aimed at a baby aged nine months and over, a toddler or small child aged eighteen months to four years, and two adults.

Eating Together

Family meal-times should be a pleasure, but they can all too often turn into a battleground. Whatever family rules you have about table manners, it's important that the family knows about them and that you are consistent. What matters to some families may not be important to you. If you want your children to stay at the table until everyone has finished, make sure everyone understands this. Some parents may feel it's more relaxing if the children leave the table once they have finished, leaving the adults to eat the rest of their meal in relative peace. Whatever you decide, stick to it, and don't be browbeaten by well-meaning grandparents or friends. Try to eat together as a family at least once a day, even if you don't all

Left: *Part of the fun of eating together is sharing the preparation, too. Children love helping in the kitchen, and this involves them in the meal from the very start.*

Below: *A relaxed but polite atmosphere will enhance enjoyment and consequently encourage good eating habits.*

eat the same food, so that your toddler can learn how to behave by watching the rest of the family. Explain to other members of the family that you are all setting an example for the baby – a great way to make everyone pull their socks up, whatever their age.

It is never too early to encourage children to help: laying (setting) the table can become quite a game, especially if dolly or teddy has a place set too. Passing plates, bread and salt and pepper can be perilous to begin with but with a little practice becomes second nature.

Transform a dull Monday meal-time into a special occasion with a few flowers or candles (well out of reach of very tiny children) and pretty table mats and paper napkins for added decoration.

Be careful if using a tablecloth when eating with very young children, as they can pull the cloth and everything with it on to the floor and themselves, with serious consequences if there's hot food or drinks around.

Above: *Laying the table is another task that children delight in, and another way to make them feel part of the family meal-time.*

Below: *Even if the child is too young to have exactly the same food, sharing the table is important.*

Similarly, beware of tiny hands reaching out from the high-chair to grab a mug of hot coffee or snatch a sharp knife.

Offer a variety of foods at each meal, some foods you know your toddler and baby will like and foods that you like too, so that everyone is happy. Offer very tiny portions of foods that are new or ones that your child is not very keen on, and encourage your child to have at least one mouthful.

Encourage the baby to feed herself with easy-to-pick-up finger foods. This gives the adults a chance to eat their food, too. Don't worry about the mess until you get to the end of the meal.

For added protection when your toddler is eating at the table, use a wipe-clean place mat and cover the seat of the dining chair with a towel or dish towel. Better still, buy a thin padded seat cover that is removable and machine-washable but will tie on to the seat securely.

Children cannot bear to eat foods that are too hot, not just because they may burn their mouth, but because of the frustration. Not being able to eat when the food is there and they are hungry can lead to great outbursts of temper. Many children actually prefer their food to be just lukewarm. Cool broccoli quickly by rinsing with a little cold water. Spoon hot casseroles on to a large plate so they cool quickly, and always test the temperature of foods before serving to a child.

TABLE MANNERS

Toddlers can be incredibly messy, but try not to be too fussy and just wipe sticky hands and faces at the end of the meal. Enjoyment is the key. If your child is eating her meal with enthusiasm rather than style, then that is the most important part at the beginning – table manners will come as your child becomes more experienced and adept with a knife and fork.

Be understanding and flexible, as small children have a lot to learn when they begin to join in at family meals. An active toddler has to learn how to sit still – quite an art in itself – how to hold a knife and fork and how to drink from a cup,

Below and below right: *Never forget that food and eating are meant to be fun – don't discipline the child just for the sake of it, and don't impose adult rules too quickly.*

and somehow watch what everyone else is doing and join in too.

The baby has to adapt to sitting up at the table in his high-chair and waiting for an adult to offer him a spoonful of food. Not surprisingly, there can be a few tantrums and accidents, not to mention a mess. Try not to worry. Offer a few finger foods after a bowl of minced food so that the baby can feed himself, giving you a chance to finish your own meal and tidy up.

Above: *Good manners and sharing provide the perfect atmosphere for good eating.*

Left: *Unusual and varied environments, and the different types of food that go with them, provide huge additional pleasure, and will also help to familiarize your child with situations he will encounter later.*

TIPS

• Offer cubes of cheese at the end of a meal to help counteract the potentially harmful effects of any sugary foods eaten.

• Try to encourage children to eat more fruit. Cutting it into small pieces and arranging it on a plate can prove very inviting.

• Encourage children of all ages to drink full-fat (whole) milk, either cold, warm or flavoured, as it is a valuable source of the fat-soluble vitamins A and D and the important mineral calcium, vital for healthy bones and teeth.

• If you reheat baby food in the microwave, make sure you stir it thoroughly and leave it to stand for a couple of minutes so any hot spots can even out. Always check the temperature before serving.

• Always make sure a baby is well strapped into a high-chair and never leave children unattended while eating, in case of accidents.

• Children love the novelty of eating somewhere different. If it's a nice day, why not have a picnic in the local park. If eating outside, make food up separately.

• Snacks can play a vitally important part in a young child's diet, as their growth rate is so high it can be difficult to provide sufficient calories and protein at meal-times alone.

• Make sure you coordinate main meals and snacks so that you serve different foods and so that the snacks won't take the edge off the child's appetite for the main meal of the day.

• Try to limit sweets (candies) or cakes and fatty crisps (potato chips).

• Offer slices of fresh fruit, a few raisins or dried apricots, squares of cheese, a fruit yogurt or milky drink, Marmite or smooth peanut butter on toast.

• Make food fun and allow your child to choose where she eats her snack, e.g. in the camp in the garden or at the swings.

MEATY MAIN MEALS

TRYING TO PLEASE THE WHOLE FAMILY ALL OF THE TIME CAN BE A BIT OF A TALL ORDER, ESPECIALLY WHEN TRYING TO COOK TASTY MEALS ON A BUDGET. TRY THESE DELICIOUS NEW WAYS WITH QUICK-TO-COOK MINCE AND CHOPS, PLUS A SPEEDY STIR-FRY, OR SLOW-COOK BEEF BOURGUIGNON WITH CREAMED POTATOES, OSSO BUCCO PORK WITH RICE OR LAMB HOTPOT.

Mediterranean Lamb

3 lamb chump chops

350g/12oz courgettes (zucchini)

½ yellow (bell) pepper

½ red (bell) pepper

3 tomatoes

1 garlic clove, crushed

15ml/1 tbsp clear honey

few sprigs of fresh rosemary, plus extra to garnish

15ml/1 tbsp olive oil

200g/7oz can baked beans

salt and freshly ground black pepper

crusty bread, to serve

1 Rinse the chops under cold water, pat dry, trim off fat and place in the base of a grill (broiler) pan. Trim and slice the courgettes, cut away the core and seeds from the peppers and then rinse and cut into chunky pieces. Rinse and cut the tomatoes into quarters and arrange the vegetables around the lamb.

2 Season two of the chops for the adults with garlic, honey, rosemary and salt and pepper, and drizzle oil over the vegetables.

3 Cook under a hot grill for 12–14 minutes, turning once, until the lamb is well browned and cooked through and the vegetables are browned.

4 Warm the baked beans in a small pan. Drain and transfer the unseasoned chop to a chopping board and cut away the bone and fat. Thinly slice half the meat for the toddler and arrange on a plate with a few of the vegetables and 30–45ml/ 2–3 tbsp of the baked beans.

5 Chop or process the remaining lamb with four slices of courgette, two small pieces of pepper, two peeled tomato quarters and 15–30ml/1–2 tbsp of baked beans, adding a little boiled water if too dry. Spoon into a dish for the baby and test the temperature of the children's food before serving.

6 For the adult's portions, discard the cooked rosemary. Spoon the pan juices over the chops and garnish with fresh rosemary. Serve with crusty bread.

TIP

Lamb varies in price throughout the year. Depending on the season and price you may prefer to use lamb cutlets or loin chops. Allow two chops per adult and reduce the cooking time slightly, as these chops are smaller. Do not give honey to young children.

Lamb Hotpot

350g/12oz lamb fillet

1 onion

1 carrot

175g/6oz swede (rutabaga)

15ml/1 tbsp sunflower oil

30ml/2 tbsp plain (all-purpose) flour

450ml/¾ pint/1⅞ cups lamb stock

15ml/1 tbsp fresh sage or 1.5ml/
  ¼ tsp dried

½ dessert apple

275g/10oz potatoes

15g/½oz/1 tbsp butter

225g/8oz Brussels sprouts

salt and freshly ground black pepper

1 Preheat the oven to 180°C/ 350°F/Gas 4. Rinse the lamb under cold water, pat dry, trim away any fat and then slice thinly. Peel and chop the onion, carrot and swede.

2 Heat the oil in a large frying pan and fry the lamb, turning until browned on both sides. Lift the lamb out of the pan, draining off any excess oil, and transfer one-third to a small 600ml/1 pint/2½ cup casserole dish for the children and the rest to a 1.2 litre/2 pint/5 cup casserole dish for the adults.

3 Add the vegetables to the pan and fry for 5 minutes, stirring until lightly browned.

4 Stir in the flour, then add the stock and sage. Bring to the boil, stirring, then divide between the two casserole dishes.

5 Core, peel and chop the apple and add both to the larger casserole dish with a little seasoning.

6 Thinly slice the potatoes and arrange overlapping slices over both casserole dishes. Dot with butter and season the larger dish.

7 Cover and cook in the oven for 1¼ hours. For a brown topping, remove the lid and grill (broil) for a few minutes at the end of cooking, until browned. Cook the Brussels sprouts in boiling water for 8–10 minutes, until tender, and drain.

8 Chop or process half the hotpot from the small casserole, with a few sprouts for the baby, adding extra gravy if needed, until the desired consistency is reached. Spoon into a baby dish.

9 Spoon the remaining child's hotpot on to a plate, add a few sprouts and cut up any large pieces. Test the temperature of the children's food before serving.

10 Spoon the hotpot for the adults on to serving plates and serve with Brussels sprouts.

TIP
Traditionally neck (cross rib) or scrag end of lamb would have been used for making a hotpot. This cut does require very long slow cooking and can be fatty with lots of bones so not ideal for children. Fillet of lamb is very lean, with very little waste and makes a tasty and healthier alternative.

Beef Korma

350g/12oz lean minced (ground) beef

1 onion, chopped

1 carrot, chopped

1 garlic clove, crushed

400g/14oz can tomatoes

pinch of dried mixed herbs

25g/1oz pasta shapes

50g/2oz creamed coconut or
120ml/4fl oz/½ cup coconut milk

50g/2oz button (white) mushrooms

50g/2oz fresh spinach leaves

15ml/1 tbsp hot curry paste

salt and freshly ground black pepper

boiled rice, warm naan bread and a
little grated Cheddar cheese, to serve

1 Dry fry the meat and onion in a medium-size pan, stirring until the beef has browned.

2 Add the carrot, garlic, tomatoes and herbs, bring to the boil, stirring, and then cover and simmer for about 30 minutes, stirring occasionally.

3 Cook the pasta in a small pan of boiling water for 10 minutes, until tender. Drain.

4 Meanwhile place the coconut or coconut milk in a small bowl, add 120ml/4fl oz/½ cup of boiling water and stir until dissolved. Wipe and slice mushrooms, and wash and drain spinach, discarding any large stalks.

5 Transfer one-third of the meat mixture to another pan. Stir the coconut mixture, curry paste and salt and pepper into the remaining meat mixture and cook for about 5 minutes, stirring.

6 Mash or process one-third of the pasta and reserved meat mixture to the desired consistency for the baby and spoon into a small dish.

7 Spoon the remaining pasta and reserved meat mixture into a small bowl for the older child.

8 Stir the mushrooms and spinach into the curried beef and cook for 3–4 minutes, until the spinach has just wilted. Spoon on to warmed serving plates for the adults and serve with boiled rice and warmed naan bread. Sprinkle the toddler's portion with a little grated cheese. Test the temperature of the children's food before serving.

TIPS

Weigh spinach after it has been picked over and the stalks have been removed or, buy ready-prepared spinach. If you can't get creamed coconut, use 120ml/4fl oz/½ cup coconut milk instead, or soak 25g/1oz/1 cup desiccated (dry unsweetened shredded) coconut in 150ml/¼ pint/⅔ cup boiling water for 30 minutes, then strain and use the liquid.

...obotie with Baked Potatoes and Broccoli

3 medium baking potatoes

1 onion, chopped

350g/12oz lean minced (ground) beef

1 garlic clove, crushed

10ml/2 tsp mild curry paste

10ml/2 tsp wine vinegar

90ml/6 tbsp fresh breadcrumbs

15ml/1 tbsp tomato purée (paste)

25g/1oz sultanas (golden raisins)

15ml/1 tbsp mango chutney

1 medium banana, sliced

2 eggs

20ml/4 tsp turmeric

120ml/4fl oz/½ cup skimmed milk

4 small bay leaves

225g/8oz broccoli, cut into florets

30ml/2 tbsp fromage frais or Greek (US strained plain) yogurt

200g/7oz can baked beans

salt and freshly ground black pepper

1 Preheat the oven to 180°C/ 350°F/Gas 4. Scrub the potatoes, insert a skewer into each and bake for 1½ hours, until tender.

2 Place the chopped onion and 225g/8oz of the beef in a pan and dry fry, until browned all over, stirring frequently.

3 Add the garlic and curry paste, stir well and cook for 1 minute, then remove from the heat and stir in the vinegar, 60ml/4 tbsp of the breadcrumbs, the tomato purée, sultanas and a little salt and pepper.

TIP
Serve any leftover adult portions cold with salad.

4 Chop up any large pieces of mango chutney and stir into the meat mixture with the banana slices. Spoon into a 900ml/1½ pint/3¾ cup ovenproof dish and press into an even layer with the back of a spoon.

5 Place the dish on a baking sheet, cover loosely with foil and cook for 20 minutes.

6 Meanwhile, mix the remaining beef with the remaining breadcrumbs, then beat the eggs together and stir 15ml/1 tbsp into the meat. Make eight small meatballs about the size of a grape for the baby. Form the remaining beef into a 7.5cm/3in burger, using an upturned cookie cutter as a mould.

7 Blend the turmeric, milk and a little salt and pepper with the remaining eggs. Remove the cover from the bobotie, and lay the bay leaves over the meat.

8 Pour the egg mixture over. Return to the oven for a further 30 minutes, until well risen and set.

9 When the adults' portion is ready, heat the grill (broiler) and cook the burger and meatballs until browned, turning once. The burger will take 8–10 minutes, while the meatballs will take about 5 minutes.

10 Cook the broccoli in boiling water until tender and drain.

11 Cut the bobotie for the adults into wedges and serve with baked potatoes topped with fromage frais or Greek yogurt and broccoli.

12 Serve the toddler's burger with half a potato, warmed baked beans and a few broccoli florets. Serve the baby's meatballs with chunky pieces of peeled potato and broccoli. Spoon a few baked beans into a small dish for the baby. Test the temperature of the food before serving to the children.

Moussaka

1 onion, chopped

350g/12oz minced (ground) lamb

400g/14oz can tomatoes

1 bay leaf

1 medium aubergine (eggplant), sliced

2 medium potatoes

1 medium courgette (zucchini), sliced

30ml/2 tbsp olive oil

2.5ml/½ tsp grated nutmeg

2.5ml/½ tsp ground cinnamon

2 garlic cloves, crushed

salt and freshly ground black pepper

For the Sauce

30ml/2 tbsp margarine

30ml/2 tbsp plain (all-purpose) flour

200ml/7fl oz/1 cup milk

pinch of grated nutmeg

15ml/1 tbsp freshly grated Parmesan cheese

20ml/4 tsp fresh breadcrumbs

1 Dry fry the onion and lamb in a pan until browned, stirring. Add the tomatoes and bay leaf, bring to the boil, stirring, then cover and simmer for 30 minutes.

2 Place the aubergine slices in a single layer on a baking sheet, sprinkle with a little salt and set aside for 20 minutes. Preheat oven to 200°C/400°F/Gas 6.

3 Slice the potatoes thinly and cook in boiling water for 3 minutes. Add the courgette and cook for 2 minutes, until tender.

4 Remove most of the slices with a slotted spoon and place in a colander, leaving just enough for the baby portion. Cook these for 2–3 minutes more until soft, then drain. Rinse the vegetables and drain well.

5 Rinse the salt off the aubergine and pat dry. Heat the oil in a frying pan and fry the aubergines until browned on both sides. Drain.

6 Spoon 45ml/3 tbsp of the meat mixture into a bowl with the baby vegetables and chop or purée to the desired consistency.

7 Spoon 60ml/4 tbsp of the meat mixture into an ovenproof dish for the older child. Arrange four slices of potato, a slice of aubergine and three slices of courgette on top.

8 Stir the spices, garlic and seasoning into the remaining lamb mixture, and cook for 1 minute and then spoon into a 1.2 litre/ 2 pint/5 cup shallow ovenproof dish discarding the bay leaf.

9 Arrange the remaining potatoes overlapping on top of the lamb, and then add the aubergine slices, tucking the courgette slices in between the aubergines in a random pattern.

10 To make the sauce, melt the margarine in a small pan, stir in the flour, then gradually add the milk and bring to the boil, stirring until thickened and smooth. Add a pinch of nutmeg and a little salt and pepper.

11 Pour a little of the sauce over the toddler's portion, then pour the rest over the adults' portion. Sprinkle the larger dish with Parmesan cheese and 15ml/3 tsp breadcrumbs, sprinkling the remaining breadcrumbs over the toddler's portion.

12 Cook the moussakas in the oven. The larger dish will take 45 minutes, while the toddler's portion will take about 25 minutes.

13 Reheat the baby portion, and test the temperature of the children's food before serving.

Chilli con Carne

3 medium baking potatoes

1 onion, chopped

450g/1lb lean minced (ground) beef

1 carrot, chopped

½ red (bell) pepper, cored, seeded and diced

400g/14oz can tomatoes

10ml/2 tsp tomato purée (paste)

150ml/¼ pint/⅔ cup beef stock

3 small bay leaves

30ml/2 tbsp olive oil

115g/4oz button (white) mushrooms, sliced

2 garlic cloves, crushed

10ml/2 tsp mild chilli powder

2.5ml/½ tsp ground cumin

5ml/1 tsp ground coriander

200g/7oz can red kidney beans, drained

40g/1½oz frozen mixed vegetables

15ml/1 tbsp milk

knob (pat) of butter or margarine

60ml/4 tbsp fromage frais or Greek (US strained plain) yogurt

15ml/1 tbsp chopped fresh coriander (cilantro) leaves

salt and freshly ground black pepper

green salad, to serve

1 Preheat the oven to 180°C/ 350°F/Gas 4. Scrub and prick the potatoes and cook in the oven for 1½ hours. Dry fry the onion and beef in a pan until browned. Add the carrot and red pepper and cook for 2 minutes.

2 Add the tomatoes, tomato purée and stock and bring to the boil. Transfer one quarter of the mixture to a 600ml/1 pint/2½ cup casserole dish, add 1 of the bay leaves, cover with a lid and set aside.

3 Spoon the remaining meat mixture into a 1.2 litre/2 pint/ 5 cup casserole. Heat 15ml/1 tbsp of the oil in the same pan and fry the mushrooms and garlic for 3 minutes.

4 Stir in the spices and seasoning, cook for 1 minute, then add the drained red kidney beans and the remaining bay leaves and stir into the meat mixture. Cover and cook both dishes in the oven for 1 hour.

5 When the potatoes are cooked, cut into halves or quarters and scoop out the potato, leaving a thin layer of potato on the skin.

6 Brush the potato skins with the remaining oil and grill (broil) for 10 minutes, until browned.

7 Boil the frozen mixed vegetables for 5 minutes and mash the potato centres with milk and a knob of butter or margarine.

8 Spoon the meat from the smaller casserole into an ovenproof ramekin dish for the toddler and the rest into a bowl for the baby. Top both with some of the mashed potato.

9 Drain the vegetables, arrange two pea eyes, carrot pieces for the mouth and mixed vegetables for hair on the toddler's dish.

10 Spoon the remaining vegetables into a baby bowl and chop or process to the desired consistency. Test the temperature of the children's food before serving.

11 Spoon the adults' chilli on to warmed serving plates, add the potato skins and top with fromage frais or Greek yogurt and chopped coriander. Serve with a green salad.

Beef Bourguignon with Creamed Potatoes

450g/1lb stewing beef

15ml/1 tbsp vegetable oil

1 onion, chopped

30ml/2 tbsp plain (all-purpose) flour

300ml/½ pint/1¼ cups beef stock

15ml/1 tbsp tomato purée (paste)

small bunch of fresh herbs or 1.5ml/ ¼ tsp dried

2 garlic cloves, crushed

90ml/6 tbsp red wine

75g/3oz shallots

75g/3oz button (white) mushrooms

25g/1oz/2 tbsp butter

450g/1lb potatoes

175g/6oz green cabbage

30–60ml/2–4 tbsp milk

salt and freshly ground black pepper

a few fresh herbs, to garnish

1 Preheat the oven to 160°C/ 325°F/Gas 3. Trim away any fat from the beef and cut into cubes.

2 Heat the oil in a frying pan, add half of the beef and fry until browned. Transfer to a plate and fry the remaining beef and the chopped onion until browned.

3 Return the first batch of beef to the pan with any meat juices, stir in the flour and then add the stock and tomato purée. Bring to the boil, stirring, until thickened.

4 Spoon one-third of the beef mixture into a small 600ml/ ½ pint/1¼ cup casserole dish for the children, making sure that the meat is well covered with stock. Add a few fresh herbs or half a dried bay leaf. Set the casserole aside.

5 Add the remaining herbs, garlic, wine and seasoning to the beef in the frying pan and bring to the boil. Transfer the beef to a 1.2 litre/ 2 pint/5 cup casserole dish. Cover both dishes and cook in the oven for about 2 hours, or until the meat is very tender.

6 Meanwhile, halve the shallots if they are large, wipe and slice the mushrooms, cover and put to one side.

7 Half an hour before the end of cooking, fry the shallots in a little butter until browned, then add the mushrooms and fry for 2–3 minutes. Stir into the larger casserole and cook for the remaining time.

8 Cut the potatoes into chunky pieces and cook in a pan of boiling, salted water for 20 minutes. Shred the cabbage, discarding the hard core, rinse and steam above the potatoes for the last 5 minutes.

9 Drain the potatoes and mash with 30ml/2 tbsp of the milk and the remaining butter.

10 Chop or process one-third of the child's casserole with a spoonful of cabbage, adding extra milk if necessary. Spoon into a dish for the baby, with a little potato.

11 Spoon the remaining child's casserole on to a plate for the toddler. Remove any bay leaf and cut up any large pieces of beef. Add potato and cabbage.

12 Garnish the adults' casserole with fresh herbs and serve with potatoes and cabbage. Test the temperature of the children's food.

Osso Bucco Pork with Rice

3 pork spare rib chops, about 500g/
1¼lb

15ml/1 tbsp olive oil

1 onion, chopped

1 large carrot, chopped

2 celery sticks, thinly sliced

2 garlic cloves, crushed

400g/14oz can tomatoes

few sprigs fresh thyme or 1.5ml/
¼ tsp dried

grated rind and juice of ½ lemon

150g/5oz/⅔ cup long grain rice

pinch of turmeric

115g/4oz green beans

knob (pat) of butter

20ml/4 tbsp freshly grated Parmesan
cheese

salt and freshly ground black pepper

1 or 2 sprigs parsley

1 Preheat the oven to 180°C/
350°F/Gas 4. Rinse the chops
under cold water and pat dry.

2 Heat the oil in a large frying pan,
add the pork, brown on both
sides and transfer to a casserole dish.

3 Add the onion, carrot and celery
to the frying pan and fry for
3 minutes, until lightly browned.

4 Add half the garlic, the
tomatoes, thyme and lemon
juice and bring to the boil, stirring.
Pour the mixture over the pork,
cover and cook in the oven for 1½
hours, or until tender.

5 Half fill two small pans with water
and bring to the boil. Add
115g/4oz/½ cup rice to one with a
pinch of turmeric and salt, add the
remaining rice to the second pan.
Return to the boil, and simmer.

6 Trim the beans and steam above
the larger pan of rice for 8
minutes, or until the rice is tender.

7 Drain both pans of rice, return
the yellow rice to the pan and
add the butter, Parmesan cheese and a
little pepper. Mix together well and
keep warm.

8 Dice one chop, discarding any
bone if necessary. Spoon a little
of the white rice on to a plate for the
toddler and add half of the diced
chop. Add a few vegetables and a
spoonful of the sauce. Process the
other half of chop, some vegetables,
rice and sauce to the desired
consistency and turn into a small
bowl for the baby.

9 Spoon the yellow rice on to the
adults' plates and add a pork
chop to each. Season the sauce to
taste and then spoon the sauce and
vegetables over the meat, discarding
the thyme sprigs if used. Finely chop
the parsley and sprinkle over the
pork with the lemon rind and the
remaining crushed garlic.

10 Serve the adults' and
toddler's portions with green
beans. Test the temperature of the
children's food before serving.

Pork Stir-fry

250g/9oz pork fillet (tenderloin)

1 courgette (zucchini)

1 carrot

½ green (bell) pepper

½ red (bell) pepper

½ yellow (bell) pepper

200g/7oz packet fresh beansprouts

20ml/4 tsp vegetable oil

25g/1 oz cashew nuts

150ml/¼ pint/⅔ cup chicken stock

30ml/2 tbsp tomato ketchup

10ml/2 tsp cornflour (cornstarch), blended with 15ml/1 tbsp cold water

1 garlic clove, crushed

10ml/2 tsp soy sauce

20ml/4 tsp yellow bean paste or hoisin sauce

1 Rinse the pork under cold water, cut away any fat and thinly slice. Halve the courgette lengthways, then thinly slice the carrot, and cut the peppers into strips, discarding the core and the seeds. Place the beansprouts in a sieve (strainer) and rinse well.

2 Heat 15ml/3 tsp of the oil in a wok or large frying pan, add the cashews and fry for 2 minutes, until browned. Drain and reserve.

3 Add the sliced pork and stir-fry for 5 minutes, until browned all over and cooked through. Drain and keep warm.

4 Add the remaining oil and stir-fry the courgette and carrot for 2 minutes. Add the peppers and fry for a further 2 minutes.

5 Stir in the beansprouts, stock, ketchup and the cornflour mixture, bring to the boil, stirring until the sauce has thickened.

6 Transfer 1 large spoonful of the vegetables to a bowl and 2–3 large spoonfuls to a plate for the children and set aside. Add the garlic and soy sauce to the pan and cook for 1 minute.

7 Chop or process four slices of pork with the baby's reserved vegetables to the desired consistency and turn into a baby bowl. Arrange six slices of pork on the toddler's plate with the reserved vegetables. Spoon the vegetables in the wok on to two adult serving plates.

8 Return the remaining pork to the wok with the nuts and yellow bean paste or hoisin sauce and cook for 1 minute. Spoon on to the adults' plates and serve immediately. Test the temperature of the children's food before serving.

Sausage Casserole

450g/1lb large sausages

15ml/1 tbsp vegetable oil

1 onion, chopped

225g/8oz carrots, chopped

400g/14oz can mixed beans in water, drained

15ml/1 tbsp plain (all-purpose) flour

450ml/¾ pint/1⅞ cup beef stock

15ml/1 tbsp Worcestershire sauce

15ml/3 tsp tomato purée (paste)

15ml/3 tsp soft brown sugar

10ml/2 tsp Dijon mustard

1 bay leaf

1 dried chilli, chopped

3 medium baking potatoes

salt and freshly ground black pepper

butter and sprigs of fresh parsley, to serve

1 Preheat the oven to 180°C/ 350°F/Gas 4. Prick and separate the sausages.

2 Heat the oil in a frying pan, add the sausages and cook over a high heat until evenly browned but not cooked through. Drain and transfer to a plate.

3 Add the chopped onion and carrots to the pan and fry until lightly browned. Add the drained beans and flour, stir well and then spoon one-third of the mixture into a small casserole. Stir in 150ml/ ¼ pint/⅔ cup stock, 5ml/1 tsp tomato purée and 5ml/1 tsp sugar.

4 Add the Worcestershire sauce, remaining beef stock, tomato purée and sugar to the pan, together with the mustard, bay leaf and chopped chilli. Season and bring to the boil, then pour the mixture into a large casserole.

5 Add two sausages to the small casserole and the rest to the larger dish. Cover both and cook in the oven for 1½ hours.

6 Scrub and prick the potatoes and cook on a shelf above the casserole for 1½ hours, until tender.

7 Spoon two-thirds of the child's casserole on to a plate for the toddler. Slice the sausages and give her two-thirds. Halve one of the baked potatoes, add a knob (pat) of butter and place on the toddler's plate.

8 Scoop the potato from the other half and mash or process with the remaining child's beans to the desired consistency for the baby. Spoon into a dish and serve the remaining sausage slices as finger food.

9 Spoon the adults' casserole on to plates, halve the other potatoes, add butter and garnish with parsley. Test the temperature of the children's food.

PERFECT POULTRY

WHATEVER THE AGE OF THE DINER, CHICKEN AND TURKEY ARE ALWAYS POPULAR. AVAILABLE IN A RANGE OF CUTS AND PRICES, THERE'S SOMETHING TO SUIT ALL BUDGETS AND TASTES, FROM A TASTY SALAD TO PAN-FRIED TURKEY WITH CORIANDER, TANDOORI-STYLE CHICKEN OR CHICKEN WRAPPERS WITH PESTO, HAM AND CHEESE.

Chicken and Thyme Casserole

6 chicken thighs

15ml/1 tbsp olive oil

1 onion, chopped

30ml/2 tbsp plain (all-purpose) flour

300ml/½ pint/1¼ cups chicken stock

few sprigs fresh thyme or 1.5 ml/ ¼ tsp dried

To Serve

350g/12oz new potatoes

1 large carrot

115g/4oz/¾ cup frozen peas

5ml/1 tsp Dijon mustard

grated rind and juice of ½ orange

60ml/4 tbsp fromage frais or natural (plain) yogurt

salt and freshly ground black pepper

fresh thyme or parsley, to garnish

1 Preheat the oven to 180°C/ 350°F/Gas 4. Rinse the chicken under cold water and pat dry.

2 Heat the oil in a large frying pan, add the chicken and brown on both sides, then transfer to a casserole.

3 Add the onion and fry, stirring until lightly browned. Stir in the flour, then add the stock and thyme and bring to the boil, stirring.

4 Pour over the chicken, cover and cook in the oven for 1 hour, or until tender.

5 Meanwhile, scrub the potatoes and cut any large ones in half. Cut the carrot into matchsticks.

6 Cook the potatoes in boiling water 15 minutes before the chicken is ready and cook the carrots and peas in a separate pan of boiling water for 5 minutes. Drain.

7 Take one chicken thigh out of the casserole, remove the skin and cut the meat away from the bone. Place in a food processor or blender with some of the vegetables and gravy and chop or process to the desired consistency. Turn into a baby bowl.

8 Take a second chicken thigh out of the casserole for the toddler, remove the skin and bone and slice if necessary. Arrange on a plate with some of the vegetables and gravy. Test the temperature of the children's food before serving.

9 Arrange two chicken thighs on warmed serving plates for the adults. Stir the mustard, orange rind and juice, fromage frais or yogurt, and seasoning into the hot sauce and then spoon over the chicken. Serve at once, with the vegetables, garnished with a sprig of thyme or parsley.

Tandoori-style Chicken

6 chicken thighs

150g/5oz natural (plain) yogurt

6.5ml/1¼ tsp paprika

5ml/1 tsp hot curry paste

5ml/1 tsp coriander seeds, roughly crushed

2.5ml/½ tsp cumin seeds, roughly crushed

2.5ml/½ tsp turmeric

pinch of dried mixed herbs

5ml/2 tsp vegetable oil

To Serve

350g/12oz new potatoes

3 celery sticks

10cm/4in piece cucumber

15ml/1 tbsp olive oil

5ml/1 tsp white wine vinegar

5ml/1 tsp mint

salt and freshly ground black pepper

few sprigs of watercress, knob (pat) of butter and cherry tomatoes, to serve

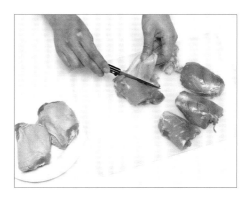

1 Cut away the skin from the chicken thighs and slash the meat two or three times with a small knife. Rinse under cold water and pat dry.

2 Place four thighs in a shallow dish, the other two on a plate. Place the yogurt, 5ml/1 tsp of the paprika, the curry paste, both seeds and almost all the turmeric into a small bowl and mix together. Spoon over the four chicken thighs.

3 Sprinkle the remaining paprika and the mixed herbs over the other chicken thighs and sprinkle the remaining pinch of turmeric over one thigh. Cover both dishes loosely with clear film (plastic wrap) and chill in the refrigerator for 2–3 hours.

4 Preheat the oven to 200°C/400°F/Gas 6. Arrange the chicken thighs on a roasting rack set over a small roasting pan and drizzle oil over the herbed chicken. Pour a little boiling water into the base of the pan and cook for 45–50 minutes, until the juices run clear when the chicken is pierced with a skewer.

5 Meanwhile, scrub the potatoes and halve any large ones. Cook in a pan of boiling water for 15 minutes, until tender.

6 Cut one celery stick and a small piece of cucumber into matchsticks. Chop or shred the remaining celery and cucumber.

7 Blend together the oil, vinegar, mint and seasoning in a bowl and add the chopped or shredded celery, cucumber and watercress, tossing well to coat.

8 Drain the potatoes and toss in a little butter. Divide the potatoes among the adults' plates, toddler's dish and the baby bowl. Cut the chicken off the bone for the toddler and arrange on a plate with half of the celery and cucumber sticks.

9 Cut the remaining chicken thigh into tiny pieces for the baby, discarding the bone, and allow to cool. Add to the bowl with the cooled potatoes and vegetable sticks and allow the baby to feed herself. Add a few halved tomatoes to each portion. Test the temperature of the children's food before serving.

10 For the adults, arrange the chicken thighs on warmed serving plates with the potatoes. Serve with the piquant salad.

Chicken Wrappers

3 boneless, skinless chicken breasts

5ml/1 tsp pesto

40g/1½oz thinly sliced ham

50g/2oz Cheddar or mild cheese

350g/12oz new potatoes

175g/6oz green beans

15g/½oz/1 tbsp butter

10ml/2 tsp olive oil

1 tomato

6 stoned (pitted) black olives

10ml/2 tsp plain (all-purpose) flour

150ml/¼ pint/⅔ cup chicken stock

15ml/1 tbsp crème fraîche or sour cream (optional)

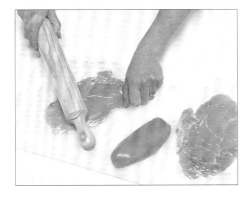

1 Rinse the chicken under cold water and pat dry. Put one chicken breast between two pieces of clear film (plastic wrap) and bat out with a rolling pin. Repeat with the other two chicken breasts.

TIP
Depending on the age of the baby, you may prefer to omit the sauce and serve the meal as finger food, cutting it into more manageable pieces first.

2 Spread pesto over two of the chicken breasts and divide the ham among all three. Cut the cheese into three thick slices, then add one to each piece of chicken. Roll up so that the cheese is completely enclosed, then secure with string.

3 Scrub the potatoes, halve any large ones and cook in a pan of boiling water for 15 minutes, until tender. Trim the beans and cook in a separate pan of boiling water for 10 minutes.

4 Meanwhile, heat the butter and oil in a large frying pan, add the chicken and cook for about 10 minutes, turning several times, until well browned and cooked through.

5 Lift the chicken out of the pan, keeping the pieces spread with pesto warm, and leaving the other one to cool slightly.

6 Cut the tomato into wedges and halve the olives. Stir in the flour and cook for 1 minute. Gradually stir in the stock and bring to the boil, stirring until thickened. Add the tomato and olives.

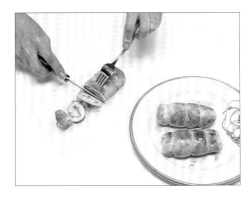

7 Snip the string off the chicken and slice the children's chicken breast thinly. Arrange four chicken slices on a child's plate with a couple of spoonfuls of sauce and a few potatoes and green beans. (Don't offer olives unless the child is a very adventurous eater.)

8 Chop or process the remaining cut chicken with 30ml/2 tbsp of the sauce, one or two potatoes and three green beans to the desired consistency. Test the temperature of the children's food before serving.

9 Arrange the remaining chicken on plates. Add the crème fraîche or sour cream to the pan, if using, and heat gently. Spoon over the chicken and serve with vegetables.

Pan-fried Turkey with Coriander

3 turkey breast steaks

1 onion

1 red (bell) pepper, cored and seeded

15ml/1 tbsp vegetable oil

5ml/1 tsp plain (all-purpose) flour

150ml/¼ pint/⅔ cup chicken stock

30ml/2 tbsp frozen corn

150g/5oz/⅔ cup long grain white rice

1 garlic clove

1 dried chilli

50g/2oz creamed coconut or
  200ml/7fl oz/1 cup coconut cream

30ml/2 tbsp chopped fresh coriander
  (cilantro)

fresh coriander sprigs, to garnish

fresh lime wedges, to serve

1 Rinse the turkey steaks under cold water, and pat dry. Chop one of the steaks, finely chop one quarter of the onion and dice one quarter of the red pepper. Heat 5ml/ 1 tsp of the oil in a small frying pan and fry the diced turkey and chopped onion until lightly browned all over.

2 Stir in the flour, add the stock, corn and chopped pepper, then bring to the boil, cover and simmer for 10 minutes.

3 Cook the long grain rice in boiling water for 8–10 minutes, or until just tender. Drain.

4 Meanwhile, process or finely chop the remaining pieces of onion and red pepper with the garlic and chilli, including the seeds if you like hot food.

5 Put the coconut into a bowl, pour on 200 ml/7fl oz/1 cup boiling water and stir until it has completely dissolved.

6 Heat the remaining oil in a large frying pan. Brown the turkey breasts on one side, turn over and add the pepper paste. Fry for 5 minutes, until the second side of the turkey has also browned.

7 Pour the coconut milk over the turkey and cook for 2–3 minutes, stirring until the sauce has thickened slightly. Sprinkle with the chopped fresh coriander.

8 Chop or process one-third of the children's portion with 30ml/ 2 tbsp of the rice until the desired consistency is reached. Spoon into a baby bowl.

9 Spoon the child's portion on to a child's plate and serve with a little rice. Test the temperature of the children's food before serving.

10 Spoon the rest of the rice on to warmed serving plates for the adults, and add the turkey and sauce. Garnish with coriander sprigs and serve with lime wedges.

Chicken Salad

3 chicken breasts, boned and skinned

½ onion, chopped

1 carrot, chopped

150ml/¼ pint/⅔ cup chicken stock

few fresh herbs or a pinch of dried mixed herbs

30ml/2 tbsp butter or margarine

15ml/1 tbsp plain (all-purpose) flour

30ml/2 tbsp frozen corn, defrosted

3 slices bread

2 celery sticks

1 green eating apple

1 red eating apple

mixed green salad leaves, to serve

For the Dressing

45ml/3 tbsp natural (plain) yogurt

45ml/3 tbsp mayonnaise

5ml/1 tsp ground coriander

salt and freshly ground black pepper

1 Rinse the chicken breasts under cold water and place in a pan with the chopped onion and carrot, stock and herbs. Cover and cook for 15 minutes, or until the chicken is cooked through.

2 Cut one chicken breast into small dice, cutting the other two into larger pieces.

3 Strain the stock into a jug (cup), finely chop the carrot and remove and discard the onion and herbs.

4 Preheat the oven to 190°C/375°F/Gas 5. Melt 15ml/1 tbsp of the butter or margarine in a small pan, stir in the flour. Gradually stir in the strained stock and bring to the boil, stirring continuously, until the sauce is thick and smooth. Add the finely diced chicken, carrot and corn.

5 Cut the bread into three 7.5cm/3in squares, cutting the trimmings into tiny shapes, using cutters. Spread both sides of the squares and one side of the tiny bread shapes with the remaining butter or margarine. Press the squares into sections of a patty tin (muffin pan).

6 Bake the small shapes in the oven for 5 minutes and the squares for 10 minutes, until crisp and golden brown all over.

7 Rinse and thinly slice the celery, and quarter, core and chop half of each of the apples.

8 To make the salad dressing, blend the yogurt, mayonnaise, ground coriander and salt and pepper in a bowl. Add the thickly diced chicken and the celery, pepper and apples, and mix together.

9 Tear the salad leaves into pieces and arrange on the adults' serving plates. Spoon the chicken salad over the salad leaves.

10 Chop or process half of the child's chicken mixture to the desired consistency for the baby and spoon into a dish with the tiny bread shapes. Reheat the remaining mixture if necessary, spoon into the bread cases and arrange on a plate for the toddler. Slice the two apple halves, cutting the peel away from a few slices and add to the children's dishes. Check the temperature before serving to the children.

FISH DINNERS

QUICK TO MAKE FOR EVERYDAY MEALS OR A SPECIAL OCCASION – HERE ARE SOME FISH RECIPES FOR ANY DAY OF THE WEEK. CHOOSE FROM FRESH, FROZEN OR CANNED FISH FOR ADDED CONVENIENCE. ENCOURAGE THE CHILDREN TO TRY HOME-MADE FISH CAKES, WITH A TASTY SAUCE FOR THE ADULTS, EYE-CATCHING FISH VOL-AU-VENTS OR COLOURFUL SALMON AND COD KEBABS.

Paella

400g/14oz cod fillet

115g/4oz fish cocktail or a mixture of prawns (shrimp), mussels and squid

15ml/1 tbsp olive oil

1 onion, chopped

1 garlic clove, crushed

150g/5oz/⅔ cup long grain white rice

pinch of saffron or turmeric

few sprigs of fresh thyme or a pinch of dried thyme

225g/8oz can tomatoes

½ red (bell) pepper, cored, seeded and chopped

½ green (bell) pepper, cored, seeded and chopped

50g/2oz frozen peas

30ml/2 tbsp fresh chopped parsley

salt and freshly ground black pepper

1 Remove any skin from the cod and place the fish cocktail in a sieve (strainer) and rinse well with cold water.

2 Heat the oil in a frying pan, add the onion and fry until lightly browned, stirring occasionally. Add the garlic and 115g/4oz/½ cup of the rice and cook for 1 minute.

3 Add the saffron or turmeric, thyme, 2 of the canned tomatoes, 350ml/12fl oz/1½ cups water, and salt and pepper. Bring to the boil and cook for 5 minutes.

4 Put the remaining rice and canned tomatoes in a small pan with 90ml/3fl oz/⅓ cup water. Cover the pan and cook for about 5 minutes.

5 Add 15ml/1 tbsp of the mixed peppers and 15ml/1 tbsp of the frozen peas to the small pan, adding all the remaining vegetables to the large pan. Place 115g/4oz of the fish in a metal sieve (strainer), cutting in half if necessary. Place above a small pan of boiling water, cover and steam for 5 minutes. Add the remaining fish to the paella in the large pan, cover the pan and cook for 5 minutes.

6 Add the fish cocktail to the paella, cover the pan and cook for a further 3 minutes.

7 Stir the chopped parsley into the paella and spoon on to two warmed serving plates for the adults. Spoon half of the tomato rice mixture and half the fish on to a plate for the child and process the remaining fish and rice to the desired consistency for the baby. Spoon into a dish and check both children's meals for bones. Test the temperature of the children's food before serving.

Fish Cakes

450g/1lb potatoes, cut into pieces

450g/1lb cod fillet

75g/3oz prepared spinach leaves

75ml/5 tbsp full-fat (whole) milk

25g/1oz/2 tbsp butter

1 egg

50g/2oz/1 cup fresh breadcrumbs

25g/1oz drained sun-dried tomatoes

25g/1oz drained stuffed olives

115g/4oz Greek (US strained plain) yogurt

3 tomatoes, cut into wedges

½ small onion, thinly sliced

15ml/1 tbsp frozen peas, cooked

vegetable oil, for frying

salt and pepper

lemon and tomato wedges, sliced onion and green salad, to serve

1 Half fill a large pan or steamer base with water, add the potatoes and bring to the boil. Place the cod in a steamer top or in a colander above the pan. Cover and cook for 8–10 minutes, or until the fish flakes easily when pressed.

2 Take the fish out of the steamer and place on a plate. Add the spinach to the steamer, cook for 3 minutes, until just wilted, and transfer to a dish. Test the potatoes, cook for 1–2 minutes more if necessary, then drain and mash with 30ml/2 tbsp of the milk and the butter.

3 Peel away the skin from the fish, and break into small flakes, carefully removing any bones. Chop the spinach and add to the potato with the fish.

4 For the baby, spoon 45ml/3 tbsp of the mixture into a bowl and mash with another 30ml/2 tbsp of milk. Add a little salt and pepper, if liked, to the remaining fish mixture.

5 For the older child, shape three tablespoons of mixture into three small rounds with floured hands. For the adults, shape the remaining mixture into four cakes.

TIP

Make sure you remove all bones from the fish.

6 Beat the egg and the remaining milk on a plate. Place the breadcrumbs on a second plate and dip both the toddler and the adult fish cakes first into the egg and then into the crumb mixture.

7 Chop the sun-dried tomatoes and stuffed olives and stir into the yogurt with a little salt and pepper. Spoon into a small dish.

8 Heat some oil in a frying pan and fry the small cakes for 2–3 minutes on each side until browned. Drain well and arrange on a child's plate. Add tomato wedges for tails and peas for eyes.

9 Fry the adult fish cakes, in more oil if necessary, for 3–4 minutes on each side, until browned and heated through. Drain and serve with the dip, lemon and tomato wedges, thinly sliced onion and a green salad. Reheat the baby portion if necessary, but test the temperature of the children's food before serving.

Fish Vol-au-Vents

250g/9oz puff pastry, thawed if frozen

a little flour

beaten egg, to glaze

350g/12oz cod fillet

200ml/7fl oz/⅓ cup milk

½ leek

30ml/2 tbsp margarine

30ml/2 tbsp plain (all-purpose) flour

50g/2oz fresh prawns (shrimp)

salt and pepper

broccoli, young carrots and mangetouts (snow peas), to serve

1 Preheat the oven to 220°C/ 425°F/Gas 7. Roll out the pastry on a lightly floured surface to make a rectangle 23 × 15cm/9 × 6in. Cut into three 7cm/3in wide strips.

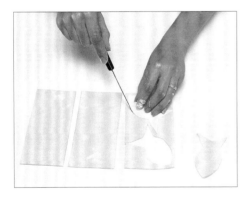

2 Cut two fish shapes from one strip. Knock up edges with a knife and cut an oval shape just in from the edge and almost through to the bottom of the pastry. Place the fish shape on a wet baking tray.

TIP
You may find it easier to cut a fish shape out of paper and then use this as a template on the pastry.

3 Neaten the edges of the remaining pastry strips, then cut smaller rectangles 1cm/½in in from the edge of both and remove.

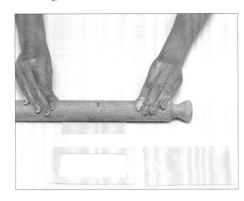

4 Roll out the smaller rectangles to the same size as the pastry frames. Brush the edges with a little egg and place the frames on top.

5 Transfer to the baking sheet. Knock up the edges of both rectangles with a small knife and flute between finger and thumb. Repeat the whole process with the third strip of pastry.

6 Stamp out tiny fish shapes from the pastry trimmings, re-rolling if necessary, and place on the baking sheet. Brush the top of the vol-au-vents with beaten egg and cook for 10 minutes. Remove the small fish and cook the larger vol-au-vents for a further 5 minutes, until they are well risen and golden brown.

7 Meanwhile make the filling. Cut the fish in two and put in a pan with the milk. Halve the leek lengthways, wash thoroughly, then slice and add to the pan.

8 Cover and simmer for 6–8 minutes, or until the fish flakes easily when pressed with a knife. Lift out of the pan, peel away the skin and then break into pieces, removing and discarding any bones.

9 Strain the milk, reserving the leeks. Melt the margarine, stir in the flour and then gradually add in the milk and bring to the boil, stirring until thick and smooth.

10 Stir the fish into the sauce. Scoop out the centres of the fish-shaped vol-au-vents and fill with a little mixture. Spoon 30ml/2 tbsp of fish mixture into a baby bowl.

11 Add a prawn to each fish-shaped vol-au-vent and stir the rest into the pan with the leeks and a little seasoning. Heat gently and spoon into the two large pastry cases (pie shells). Transfer to plates and serve with steamed vegetables.

12 Chop the baby portion with some vegetables, and serve this with some tiny pastry fishes, if wished, in a small bowl. Check the temperature of the children's food before serving.

Salmon and Cod Kebabs

200g/7oz salmon steak

275g/10oz cod fillet

15ml/3 tsp lemon juice

10ml/2 tsp olive oil

2.5ml/½ tsp Dijon mustard

350g/12oz new potatoes

200g/7oz frozen peas

50g/2oz/4 tbsp butter

15–30ml/1–2 tbsp milk

3 tomatoes, chopped, seeds discarded

¼ round (butterhead) lettuce, finely shredded

salt and freshly ground black pepper

For the Mustard Sauce

1 sprig fresh dill

20ml/4 tsp mayonnaise

5ml/1 tsp Dijon mustard

5ml/1 tsp lemon juice

2.5ml/½ tsp soft dark brown sugar

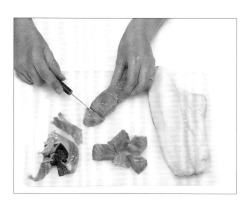

1 Rinse the fish under cold water and pat dry. Cut the salmon steak in half, cutting around the central bone. Cut away the skin and then cut into chunky cubes, making sure you remove any bones. Remove the skin from the cod and cut into similar sized pieces.

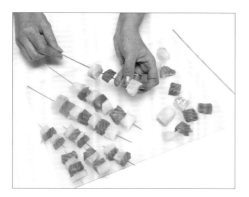

2 Cut a few pieces of fish into smaller pieces and thread on to five cocktail sticks (toothpicks). Thread the remaining fish pieces on to long wooden skewers.

3 Mix together the lemon juice, oil, Dijon mustard and a little salt and pepper to taste in a small bowl and set aside.

4 Finely chop the dill and place in a bowl with the other sauce ingredients and mix. Set aside.

5 Scrub the potatoes, halve any large ones and then cook in lightly salted water for 15 minutes, or until tender. Place the peas and half of the butter in a frying pan, cover and cook very gently for 5 minutes.

6 Preheat the grill (broiler), place the kebabs on a baking sheet and brush the larger kebabs with the lemon, oil and mustard mixture. Grill (broil) for 5 minutes, until the fish is cooked, turning once.

7 Remove the fish from two cocktail sticks and mix in a small bowl with a few new potatoes and 15ml/1 tbsp of the peas. Chop or process with a little milk until the desired consistency is reached, then transfer to a baby bowl.

8 Arrange the toddler's kebabs on a small serving plate with a few potatoes, 30ml/2 tbsp peas and a small amount of chopped tomato. Remove the cocktail sticks from the kebabs before serving.

9 Add the tomatoes to the remaining peas and cook for 2 minutes, then stir in the shredded lettuce and cook for 1 minute. Spoon on to serving plates for the adults, add the kebabs and potatoes, and serve.

CAUTION

For younger toddlers, it would be safer to remove the cocktail sticks before serving.

Tuna Florentine

50g/2oz pasta shapes

175g/6oz fresh spinach leaves

50g/2oz frozen mixed vegetables

200g/7oz can tuna in brine

2 eggs

buttered toast and grilled (broiled) tomatoes, to serve

For the Sauce

25g/1oz/2 tbsp margarine

45ml/3 tbsp plain (all-purpose) flour

300ml/½ pint/1¼ cups milk

50g/2 oz/½ cup grated Cheddar or mild cheese

1 Cook the pasta in boiling water for 10 minutes. Meanwhile, tear off any spinach stalks, wash the leaves in plenty of cold water and place in a steamer or colander.

2 Stir the frozen vegetables into the pasta as it is cooking, and then place the spinach in the steamer over the top. Cover and cook for the last 3 minutes, or until the spinach has just wilted.

TIP
Frozen vegetables are usually more nutritious than fresh vegetables, as they are frozen at their peak of perfection – they're a great time-saver too.

3 Drain the pasta and vegetables through a sieve (strainer). Chop one quarter of the spinach and add to the pasta and vegetables, dividing the remainder between two shallow 300ml/½ pint/1¼ cup ovenproof dishes for the adults.

4 Drain the tuna and divide among the dishes and sieve (strain).

5 Refill the pasta pan with water, bring to the boil, then break the eggs into the water and gently simmer until the egg whites are set. Remove the eggs with a slotted spoon, trim the whites and shake off all the water. Arrange the eggs on top of the tuna for the adults.

6 To make the sauce, melt the margarine in a small pan, stir in the flour, then gradually add the milk and bring to the boil, stirring until thick and smooth.

7 Stir the cheese into the sauce, reserving a little for the topping. Spoon the sauce over the adults' portions until the eggs are covered. Stir the children's pasta, vegetables and tuna into the remaining sauce and mix together.

8 Spoon the pasta on to a plate for the toddler and chop or process the remainder for the baby, adding a little extra milk, if necessary, to make the desired consistency. Spoon into a dish. Test the temperature of the children's food before serving.

9 Preheat the grill (broiler), sprinkle the adults' portions with the reserved cheese and grill for 4–5 minutes, until browned. Serve with buttered toast and grilled (broiled) tomatoes.

VEGETABLE FEASTS

MORE AND MORE OF US ARE OPTING TO EAT LESS MEAT FOR EITHER HEALTH OR BUDGETARY REASONS. EATING LESS MEAT DOESN'T MEAN LOSING OUT ON FLAVOUR – FAR FROM IT! CHOOSE FROM MEALS SUCH AS PENNE WITH TOMATO SAUCE, CHEESE AND VEGETABLE CRUMBLE OR SLOW-COOKED, SPICED VEGETABLE TAGINE.

Cheese on Toast

2 thick slices bread

2 thin slices bread

butter or margarine, for spreading

5ml/1 tsp Marmite (optional)

2 thin slices ham

1 garlic clove, halved

15ml/1 tbsp olive oil

200g/7oz Cheddar or mild cheese

1 tomato

6 stoned (pitted) black olives

15ml/1 tbsp chopped fresh basil

a few red onion slices

cucumber sticks and green salad, to
  serve (optional)

2 Drizzle the oil over the thick slices of toast, then rub with the cut surface of the garlic.

4 Slice the tomato and halve the olives. Arrange on the thick toast for the adults, season with pepper and add basil and onion.

3 Thinly slice the cheese and place over all of the pieces of toast.

5 Grill until the cheese is bubbly. Cut the plain cheese on toast into tiny squares, discarding crusts. Arrange on a small plate for the baby and allow to cool. Cut the Marmite and/or ham-topped toast into triangles and arrange on a plate. Add cucumber sticks to the toddler's portion and test the temperature before serving.

6 Slice the adults' toast and arrange on plates, with a green salad if liked, and serve.

1 Toast all the bread and spread the thin slices with butter or margarine. Spread one slice with Marmite, if using, and top this with ham.

Penne with Tomato Sauce

150g/5oz penne or small pasta quills

1 onion

2 celery sticks

1 red (bell) pepper

15ml/1 tbsp olive oil

1 garlic clove, crushed

400g/14oz can tomatoes

2.5ml/½ tsp caster (superfine) sugar

8 stoned (pitted) black olives

10ml/2 tsp pesto

1.5ml/¼ tsp dried chilli seeds (optional)

50g/2oz/½ cup grated Cheddar or mild cheese

salt and freshly ground black pepper

10ml/2 tsp freshly grated Parmesan cheese, to serve

green salad, to serve (optional)

1 Cook the pasta in salted boiling water for about 10–12 minutes, until just tender.

2 Meanwhile, chop the onion and the celery. Cut the pepper in half, then scoop out the core and seeds and dice the pepper finely.

3 Heat the oil in a second pan, add the vegetables and garlic and fry for 5 minutes, stirring until lightly browned.

4 Add the tomatoes and sugar and cook for 5 minutes, stirring occasionally, until the tomatoes are broken up and pulpy.

5 Drain the pasta, return to the pan and stir in the tomato sauce.

6 Spoon 45–60ml/3–4 tbsp of the mixture into a bowl or processor and chop or process to the desired consistency for the baby. Spoon 75–90ml/5–6 tbsp of the mixture into a bowl for the toddler.

7 Quarter the olives and stir into the remaining pasta with the pesto, chilli seeds if using, and a little salt and pepper. Spoon into dishes.

8 Sprinkle the grated cheese over all the dishes, and serve the adults' portions with the Parmesan cheese, and a green salad if wished. Test the temperature of the children's food before serving.

Courgette Gougère

50g/2oz/4 tbsp butter

65g/2½oz plain (all-purpose) flour

2 eggs

2.5ml/½ tsp Dijon mustard

115g/4oz Cheddar or mild cheese

salt and pepper

For the Filling

15ml/1 tbsp olive oil

350g/12oz courgettes (zucchini), sliced

1 small onion, chopped

115g/4oz button (white) mushrooms, sliced

225g/8oz tomatoes, skinned and chopped

1 garlic clove, crushed

20ml/4 tsp chopped fresh basil

1 Preheat the oven to 220°C/425°F/ Gas 7 and grease a large baking sheet. Place the butter in a medium pan with 150ml/¼ pint/⅔ cup water. Heat gently until the butter has melted, then bring to the boil.

2 Remove the pan from the heat and quickly add the flour, stir well, then return to the heat and cook for 1–2 minutes, stirring constantly until the mixture forms a smooth ball. Leave to cool for 10 minutes.

3 Beat the eggs, mustard and a little salt and pepper together. Cut 25g/1oz of the cheese into small cubes and grate the rest.

4 Add 50g/2oz of the grated cheese to the dough and then gradually beat in the eggs to make a smooth, glossy paste.

5 Spoon the mixture into a large piping (pastry) bag fitted with a medium plain nozzle. Pipe whirls close together on the baking sheet to make an 18cm/7in circular shape.

6 Pipe the remaining mixture into small balls for the baby and into the older child's initials.

7 Sprinkle the top with the remaining grated cheese.

8 Bake for 15–18 minutes for the small shapes and 25 for the ring, until well risen and browned.

9 Heat the oil in a frying pan, add the courgettes and onion, and fry until lightly browned. Add the mushrooms, fry for a further 2 minutes and then add the tomatoes. Cover and simmer for 5 minutes, until the vegetables are cooked.

10 Spoon a little mixture into the baby's bowl or into a food processor, and chop or process to the desired consistency. Serve with a few cheese balls and a little diced cheese.

11 Spoon a little on to a plate for the toddler, add an initial and the remaining diced cheese. Test the temperature of the children's food before serving.

12 Transfer the cheese ring to a serving plate and split in half horizontally. Stir the garlic, basil and a little extra seasoning into the courgette mixture and heat through. Spoon over the bottom half of the cheese ring and add the top half. Serve the gougère immediately.

TIP

Beat the gougère mixture, cheese and eggs together in a food processor, if preferred.

Cheese Vegetable Crumble

1 onion

225g/8oz carrot

175g/6oz swede (rutabaga)

175g/6oz parsnip

15ml/1 tbsp olive oil

220g/7½oz can red kidney beans

10ml/2 tsp paprika

5ml/1 tsp ground cumin

15ml/1 tbsp plain (all-purpose) flour

300ml/½ pint/1¼ cups vegetable stock

225g/8oz broccoli, to serve

For the Topping

115g/4oz Cheddar or mild cheese

50g/2oz wholemeal (whole-wheat) flour

50g/2oz plain (all-purpose) flour

50g/2oz margarine

30ml/2 tbsp sesame seeds

25g/1oz blanched almonds

salt and freshly ground black pepper

1 Preheat the oven to 190°C/ 375°F/Gas 5. Peel and roughly chop the onion. Then peel and cut the carrot, swede and parsnip into small cubes. Heat the oil in a large pan and fry the vegetables for 5 minutes, stirring until lightly browned.

2 Drain the kidney beans and add to the pan with the spices and flour. Stir well, add the stock, then cover and simmer for 10 minutes.

3 Meanwhile, make the topping. Cut a few squares of cheese for the baby and grate the rest. Put the two flours in a bowl, add the margarine and rub in with your fingertips until the mixture resembles fine breadcrumbs. Stir in the grated cheese and sesame seeds.

4 Spoon a little of the vegetable mixture into a 300ml/½ pint/ 1¼ cup ovenproof dish for the toddler. Spoon the remaining mixture into a 900ml/1½ pint/ 3¾ cup ovenproof pie dish for the adults, leaving a little vegetable mixture in the pan for the baby. Season the adults' portion with a little salt and pepper.

VARIATION
Lentil and Herb Crumble

Substitute canned lentils for the red kidney beans. Instead of the paprika and cumin, use 30ml/2 tbsp chopped, fresh mixed herbs. Add more fibre and nuttiness by replacing the plain (all-purpose) flour with rolled oats.

5 Spoon 45ml/3 tbsp of crumble over the older child's portion. Roughly chop the almonds, add to the remaining crumble with a little salt and pepper and spoon over the large dish. Bake in the oven for 20 minutes for the small dish, and 30 minutes for the large dish, until golden brown on top.

6 Add 90ml/3fl oz/⅓ cup water to the baby's portion, cover and cook for 10 minutes, stirring occasionally, until the vegetables are very tender. Mash or process to the desired consistency and spoon into a bowl.

7 Cut the broccoli into florets and cook for 5 minutes, or until tender; drain. Spoon the toddler's portion out of the dish and on to a small plate. Serve the broccoli to all members of the family, allowing the baby to pick up and eat the broccoli and cubed cheese as finger food. Check the temperature before serving to the children.

Note: Never give whole nuts to children under five, as they may choke.

Vegetable Tagine

1 onion

225g/8oz carrots

225g/8oz swede (rutabaga)

75g/3oz prunes

20ml/4 tsp olive oil

425g/15oz can chickpeas

2.5ml/½ tsp turmeric

10ml/2 tsp plain (all-purpose) flour, plus extra for dusting

2 garlic cloves, finely chopped

450ml/¾ pint/1⅞ cups chicken stock

15ml/1 tbsp tomato purée (paste)

2cm/¾in piece fresh root ginger

2.5ml/½ tsp ground cinnamon

3 cloves

115g/4oz couscous

8 green beans

2 frozen peas

piece of tomato

knob (pat) of butter or margarine

salt and freshly ground black pepper

fresh coriander (cilantro), to garnish

1 Peel and chop the onion, and peel and dice the carrots and swede. Cut the prunes into chunky pieces, discarding the stones (pits).

2 Heat 15ml/3 tsp of the olive oil in a large pan, add the onion and fry until lightly browned. Stir in the carrots and swede and fry for 3 minutes, stirring.

3 Drain the chickpeas and stir into the pan with the turmeric, flour and garlic. Add 300ml/½ pint/1¼ cup of the stock, the tomato purée, and the prunes. Bring to the boil, cover and simmer for 20 minutes, stirring occasionally.

4 Place three heaped spoonfuls of mixture in a bowl or food processor, draining off most of the liquid. Mash or process and then form the mixture into a burger with floured hands.

5 Chop or process two heaped spoonfuls of mixture and sauce to the desired consistency for the baby and spoon into a bowl.

6 Finely chop the root ginger and stir into the remaining vegetable mixture with the cinnamon, cloves, remaining stock and seasoning.

7 Place the couscous in a sieve (strainer), rinse with boiling water and fluff up the grains with a fork. Place the sieve above the vegetables, cover and steam for 5 minutes.

8 Fry the veggie burger in the remaining oil until browned on both sides. Trim and cook the beans and peas for 5 minutes. Drain and arrange on a plate like an octopus, with a piece of tomato for a mouth and peas for eyes.

9 Stir the butter or margarine into the couscous and fluff up the grains with a fork. Spoon on to warmed serving plates for adults, add the vegetable mixture and garnish with a sprig of coriander. Check the temperature of the children's food before serving.

Stilton and Leek Tart

175g/6oz/1½ cups plain (all-purpose) flour

75g/3oz/6 tbsp butter

1 carrot

2 slices ham

10cm/4in piece of cucumber

mixed green salad leaves, to serve

For the Filling

25g/1oz/2 tbsp butter

115g/4oz trimmed leek, thinly sliced

75g/3oz Stilton (blue) cheese, diced

3 eggs

175ml/6fl oz/¾ cup milk

40g/1½oz Cheddar or mild cheese, grated

pinch of paprika

salt and pepper

1 Put the flour in a bowl with a pinch of salt. Cut the butter into pieces and rub into the flour with your fingertips until the mixture resembles fine breadcrumbs.

2 Mix to a smooth dough with 30–35ml/6–7 tsp water, knead lightly and roll out thinly on a floured surface. Use to line an 18cm/7in flan dish, trimming round the edge and reserving the trimmings.

3 Re-roll the trimmings and then cut out six 7.5cm/3in circles, using a fluted cookie cutter. Press the pastry circles into sections of a patty tin (muffin pan) and chill all of the tarts.

4 Preheat the oven to 190°C/375°F/Gas 5. For the filling, melt the butter in a small frying pan and fry the leek for 4–5 minutes, until soft but not brown, stirring frequently. Turn into a bowl, stir in the diced Stilton, and then spread over the base of the large tart.

5 Beat the eggs and milk together in a small bowl and season with salt and pepper.

6 Divide the grated Cheddar among the small tartlet shells and pour some of the egg mixture over. Pour the remaining egg mixture over the leek and Stilton tart and sprinkle with paprika.

7 Cook the small tartlets for 15 minutes and the large tart for 30–35 minutes, until well risen and browned. Leave to cool.

8 Peel and coarsely grate the carrot. Cut the ham into triangles for "sails". Cut the ham trimmings into small strips for the baby. Cut the cucumber into matchsticks.

9 Place a spoonful of carrot, some cucumber, a small tart and some ham trimmings in the baby dish. Spread the remaining carrot on to a plate for the older child, place the tarts on top and secure the ham "sails" with cocktail sticks (toothpicks) Serve any remaining tarts the next day. Cut the large tart into wedges and serve with a mixed leaf salad.

JUST DESSERTS

NO ONE CAN RESIST A DESSERT, ALTHOUGH LOOKING AFTER A YOUNG FAMILY MAY MEAN IT'S MORE OF A WEEKEND TREAT THAN AN EVERYDAY OCCURRENCE. SPOIL THE FAMILY WITH A SELECTION OF THESE TASTY HOT AND COLD TREATS, FROM FRUITY EVE'S PUDDING AND PLUM CRUMBLE TO CHOCOLATE AND ORANGE TRIFLE OR STRAWBERRY PAVLOVA – ALL GUARANTEED TO GET THEM CLAMOURING FOR SECONDS.

Bread and Butter Pudding

3 dried apricots

45ml/3 tbsp sultanas (golden raisins)

30ml/2 tbsp sherry

7 slices white bread, crusts removed

25g/1oz/½ tbsp butter, softened

30ml/2 tbsp caster (superfine) sugar

pinch of ground cinnamon

4 eggs

300ml/½ pint/1¼ cups milk

few drops of vanilla essence (extract)

pouring cream, to serve

2 Preheat the oven to 190°C/ 375°F/Gas 5. Spread the bread with butter and cut one slice into very small triangles. Layer in a 150ml/¼ pint/⅔ cup pie dish with plain apricots and sultanas and 5ml/ 1 tsp of the sugar.

4 Beat the eggs, milk and vanilla together and pour into the ramekin and two pie dishes.

1 Chop two dried apricots and place in a small bowl with 30ml/ 2 tbsp of the sultanas and the sherry. Set aside for about 2 hours. Chop the remaining apricot and mix with the remaining sultanas.

3 Cut the remaining bread into larger triangles and layer in a 900ml/1½ pint/3¾ cup pie dish with the sherried fruits and all but 5ml/ 1 tsp of the remaining sugar, sprinkling the top with cinnamon. Put the last 5ml/1 tsp sugar in a small ramekin dish.

5 Stand the ramekin dish in a large ovenproof dish and half fill with hot water. Cook the small pie dish and the ramekin for 25–30 minutes, until the custard has just set, and the larger pudding for 35 minutes, until the bread has browned. Serve the adult portions with cream, if liked.

Eve's Pudding

500g/1¼lb cooking apples

50g/2oz/¼ cup caster (superfine) sugar

50g/2oz frozen or canned
  blackberries

For the Topping

50g/2oz/4 tbsp butter or margarine

50g/2oz/¼ cup caster (superfine) sugar

50g/2oz/⅓ cup self-raising
  (self-rising) flour

1 egg

½ lemon, rind only

15ml/1 tbsp lemon juice

icing (confectioners') sugar, for
  dusting

custard, to serve

1 Preheat the oven to 180°C/350°F/
Gas 4. Peel and slice the cooking
apples, discarding the core, and then
place in a pan with the caster sugar
and 15ml/1 tbsp water. Cover and
cook gently for 5 minutes, until
the apple slices are almost tender
but still whole.

2 Half fill a 150ml/¼ pint/⅔ cup
ovenproof ramekin with apple
for the toddler and mash 30ml/2 tbsp
of apple for the baby in a small bowl.

3 Put the remaining apple slices
into a 600ml/1 pint/2½ cup
ovenproof dish. Sprinkle the
blackberries over the apple slices.

4 To make the topping, place the
butter or margarine, sugar, flour
and egg in a bowl and beat until
smooth. Spoon a little of the
pudding mixture over the toddler's
ramekin so that the mixture is
almost to the top of the dish.

5 Half fill three petits fours cases
with the pudding mixture.

6 Grate the lemon rind and stir
with the juice into the remaining
mixture. Spoon over the large dish,
levelling the surface.

7 Put the small cakes, toddler and
adult dishes on a baking sheet and
bake in the oven for 8–10 minutes for
the small cakes, 20 minutes for the
ramekin and 30 minutes for the larger
dish, until they are well risen and
golden brown.

8 Dust the toddler's and adults'
portions with icing sugar and
leave to cool slightly before serving
with the custard. Warm the baby's
portion if liked, and test the
temperature before serving, with the
cakes taken out of their paper cases.

TIP
If you can't get blackberries, then
use raspberries instead. There's no
need to defrost before using, as
they will soon thaw when added
to the hot apple.

Orange and Strawberry Shortcakes

75g/3oz/6 tbsp plain (all-purpose) flour

50g/2oz/4 tbsp butter

25g/1oz/2 tbsp caster (superfine) sugar

grated rind of ½ orange

extra sugar, for sprinkling

For the Filling

175g/6oz Greek (US strained plain) yogurt

15ml/1 tbsp icing (confectioners') sugar

250g/9oz strawberries

5ml/1 tsp Cointreau (optional)

2 sprigs of fresh mint, to decorate

1 Preheat the oven to 180°C/350°F/ Gas 4. Place the flour in a bowl, cut the butter into pieces, and rub into the flour with your fingertips until the mixture resembles fine breadcrumbs.

2 Stir in the sugar and orange rind and mix to a dough.

3 Knead the dough lightly, then roll out on a floured surface to 5mm/¼in thickness. Stamp out four 9cm/3½in flower shapes or fluted rounds with a cookie cutter, and 12 small car, train or other fun shapes with novelty cutters, re-rolling the dough as necessary.

4 Place the shapes on a baking sheet, prick with a fork and sprinkle with a little extra sugar. Bake in the oven for 10–12 minutes, until pale golden, then leave to cool on the baking sheet.

5 For the filling, blend the yogurt with the sugar and wash and hull the strawberries. Pat dry. Reserve eight of the strawberries and process or liquidize the rest. Press through a sieve (strainer) and discard the seeds.

6 For the adults, put 45ml/3 tbsp of the yogurt in a bowl and stir in the Cointreau, if using. Slice four strawberries and halve two, place on a plate and cover.

7 For the toddler, slice two of the strawberries and arrange in a ring on a small plate. Spoon 30ml/ 2tbsp of yogurt into the centre of the ring and serve with three of the small biscuit (cookie) shapes.

8 For the baby, stir 15ml/1 tbsp of the strawberry purée into the remaining natural yogurt and spoon into a small dish. Serve with one or two of the small biscuit shapes.

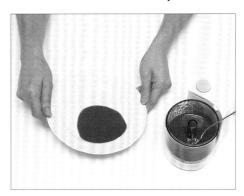

9 To complete the adults' portions, spoon purée over two plates to cover completely.

10 Spoon the reserved yogurt over two biscuits, add the sliced strawberries and top with the other two biscuits. Arrange on plates and decorate with halved strawberries and tiny sprigs of mint.

TIP
If you find shortbread difficult to roll out, then chill for 20 minutes. Knead lightly and roll out on a surface dusted with flour, dusting the rolling pin too.

Exotic Fruit Brûlée

oil, for greasing

30ml/2 tbsp demerara (raw) sugar

1 ripe mango

1 kiwi fruit

1 passion fruit

30ml/2 tbsp icing (confectioners') sugar

350g/12oz Greek (US strained plain)
  yogurt

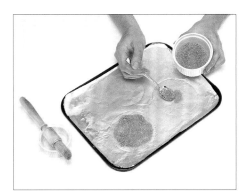

1 Line a baking sheet with foil, then with a pencil draw round the tops of two 250ml/8fl oz/1 cup ramekin dishes and one 150ml/¼ pint/⅔ cup ramekin dish. Lightly brush with oil. Sprinkle the sugar inside each marked circle in an even layer.

2 Grill the sugar discs for 2–3 minutes, or until the sugar has melted and caramelized. Leave the discs to cool on the baking sheet.

3 Slice the mango on either side of the central stone (pit) and then cut six thin slices for decoration, cutting away the skin. Cut the rest of the mango flesh from the stone, removing the skin, and finely chop one quarter, dividing between the baby bowl and small ramekin. Roughly chop the remainder and divide between the larger ramekins.

4 Peel the kiwi fruit, cut in half lengthways and then slice thinly. Reserve four half slices for decoration and divide the remaining fruit among the dishes, finely chopping the fruit for the baby and toddler. Cut the passion fruit in half and, using a teaspoon, scoop out and place the seeds in the adults' dishes.

5 Stir the icing sugar into the yogurt and mix 15ml/1 tbsp into the baby's portion. Spoon 30ml/2 tbsp yogurt over the toddler's dish and level the surface with a spoon.

6 Spoon the remaining yogurt into the other two ramekins, level the surface with a spoon and chill all of them until required.

7 When ready to serve, place the larger ramekins on two plates with the reserved mango and kiwi slices arranged around the sides. Peel the sugar discs off the foil and set on top of the adult and toddler portions. Serve the brulées immediately.

TIP
Traditionally, the sugar topping on a brulée is made by sprinkling demerara sugar over the top of the dessert and then grilling (broiling), or by making a caramel syrup and then pouring it over the dessert. Making the topping on oiled foil is by far the easiest and most foolproof way. Add the cooled sugar discs at the very last minute so that they stay crisp and you get that wonder-ful mix of crunchy sugar, velvety yogurt and refreshing fruit.

Plum Crumble

450g/1lb ripe red plums

25g/1oz/2 tbsp caster (superfine) sugar

For the Topping

115g/4oz/1 cup plain (all-purpose) flour

50g/2oz/4 tbsp butter, cut into
  pieces

25g/1oz/2 tbsp caster (superfine) sugar

10ml/2 tsp chocolate dots

75g/3oz marzipan

30ml/2 tbsp rolled oats

30ml/2 tbsp flaked (sliced) almonds

custard, to serve

1 Preheat the oven to 190°C/
375°F/Gas 5. Wash the plums,
cut into quarters and remove the
stones (pits). Place in a pan with the
sugar and 30ml/2 tbsp water, cover
and simmer for 10 minutes.

2 Drain and spoon six plum
quarters on to a chopping board
and chop finely. Spoon the plums
into a small baby dish with a little
juice from the pan.

3 Drain and roughly chop six
more of the plum quarters and
place in a 150ml/¼ pint/⅔ cup
ovenproof ramekin dish with a little
of the juice from the pan.

4 Spoon the remaining plums into
a 750ml/1¼ pint/3⅔ cup
ovenproof dish for the adults.

5 Make the topping. Place the
flour in a bowl, rub in the butter
and then stir in the sugar.

6 Mix 45ml/3 tbsp of the crumble
mixture with the chocolate dots,
then spoon over the ramekin.

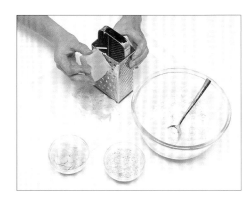

7 Coarsely grate the marzipan and
stir into the remaining crumble
with the oats and almonds. Spoon
over the adults' portion.

8 Place the toddler and adult
portions on a baking sheet and
cook for 20–25 minutes, until golden
brown. Leave to cool slightly before
serving. Warm the baby's portion if
liked and check the temperature of
the children's food before serving.
Serve with custard.

TIP
Ovens can vary in temperature:
with fan-assisted ovens you may
need to cover the adults' dish with
foil halfway through cooking to
prevent overbrowning.

Vary the fruits: cooking apples,
peaches and pears also work well.
If the plums are very sharp, you
may need to add a little extra sugar.

Chocolate and Orange Trifle

½ chocolate Swiss roll (jelly roll)

3 clementines or satsumas

20ml/4 tsp sherry

50g/2oz dark (bittersweet) chocolate

300ml/½ pint/1¼ cups ready-made custard

90ml/6 tbsp double (heavy) cream

chocolate buttons or M & M's

1 Slice the Swiss roll, halve one slice and put on a plate for the baby. Put a second slice into a ramekin dish for the older child and arrange the remaining slices in two dessert bowls for the adults.

2 Peel one clementine, separate into segments and put a few on the baby's plate. Chop the rest and add to the ramekin.

3 Peel the remaining clementines, roughly chop and add to the adults' bowls, sprinkling a little sherry over each.

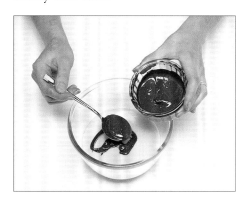

4 Break the chocolate into pieces and melt in a bowl over a pan of hot water. Stir the melted chocolate into the custard.

5 Spoon 30ml/2 tbsp of the custard into a small bowl for the baby and arrange on the plate with the Swiss roll and fruit. Spoon a little more custard into the ramekin and then add the rest to the adult dishes, smoothing the surface.

6 Whip the cream until it just holds its shape. Add a spoonful to the ramekin dish and two or three spoonfuls each to the adults' dishes, decorating each dish with sweets (candies).Chill until required.

TIPS

Chocolate may be melted in the microwave in a microwave-safe bowl for 2 minutes on Full Power (100%), stirring thoroughly halfway through cooking.

Some shops sell ready-made chocolate custard. Buy this if it's available and you're short of time.

Vary the fruits depending on what is in season, Sliced strawberries and orange, or sliced banana and fresh or canned cherries also work well.

Apple Strudel

450g/1lb cooking apples

50g/2oz dried apricots

45ml/3 tbsp sultanas (golden raisins)

30ml/2 tbsp soft light brown sugar

30ml/2 tbsp ground almonds

5ml/1 tsp ground cinnamon

25g/1oz/2 tbsp butter

150g/5oz/3 sheets filo pastry, defrosted if frozen

icing (confectioners') sugar, to dust

pouring (half-and-half) cream, to serve

1 Preheat the oven to 200°C/ 400°F/Gas 6. Peel, core and chop the apples and place 150g/5oz in a pan. Chop three apricots and add to the pan with 15ml/1 tbsp sultanas, 15ml/1 tbsp sugar and 15ml/1 tbsp water. Cover and simmer for 5 minutes.

2 Chop the remaining apricots and place in a bowl with the remaining apples, sultanas, sugar, ground almonds and cinnamon. Mix together well.

3 Melt the butter in a small pan, or microwave in a microwave-proof bowl for 30 seconds on Full Power (100%).

4 Carefully open out the pastry. Place one sheet on the work surface, brush with butter, then cover with a second sheet of pastry and brush with more butter.

5 Spoon the uncooked apple mixture in a thick band along the centre of the pastry.

6 Fold the two short sides up and over the filling and brush with butter. Fold the long sides up and over the filling, opening out the pastry and folding the pastry for an attractive finish. Place on a baking sheet and brush with a little butter.

7 Brush a little of the butter over half of the third pastry sheet, then fold the unbrushed half over the top to make a square. Brush again and cut into three equal strips.

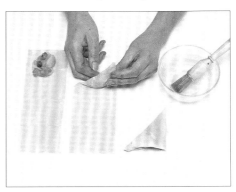

8 Put a spoonful of apple at the base of each strip, then fold the bottom right-hand corner up and over the filling, to the left side of the strip, to make a triangle.

9 Continue folding the pastry to make a triangular pasty. Repeat with the other strips.

10 Transfer to a baking sheet and brush with the remaining butter. Bake for 10 minutes, and the adults' strudel for 15 minutes, until golden and crisp. Dust with icing sugar and cool slightly.

11 Spoon the remaining cooked apple mixture into a baby dish. Mash the fruit if necessary. Transfer the toddler's portion to a plate. Slice the strudel thickly and serve with cream.

TIP

Filo pastry is usually sold frozen in 275g/10oz packets or larger. Defrost the whole pack, take out as much pastry as you need, then re-wrap the rest and return to the freezer.

Strawberry Pavlova

2 egg whites

115g/4oz caster (superfine) sugar

2.5ml/½ tsp cornflour (cornstarch)

2.5ml/½ tsp wine vinegar

For the Topping

150ml/¼ pint/⅔ cup double (heavy) cream

250g/9oz strawberries

2 chocolate dots

green jelly sweet (candy) or little pieces of angelica

1 Preheat the oven to 150°C/300°F/Gas 2 and line a baking sheet with baking parchment.

2 Whisk the egg whites until stiff and then gradually whisk in the sugar, 5ml/1 tsp at a time. Continue whisking until smooth and glossy.

3 Blend the cornflour and vinegar and fold into the egg whites.

4 Spoon the mixture into a large piping (pastry) bag fitted with a medium-size plain nozzle. Pipe six small dots for the baby and a snail for the older child with a shell about 6cm/2½in in diameter.

5 Pipe the remaining mixture into two 10cm/4in swirly circles and cook in the oven for 20–25 minutes, or until firm. Lift the meringues off the paper and leave to cool.

TIP

For perfect meringues, whisk the egg whites in a dry grease-free bowl. Remove any trace of yolk with a piece of shell and whisk until the peaks are stiff but still moist-looking. Add sugar gradually and continue whisking until very thick. Meringues may be made 1–2 days in advance. Cover with baking parchment and decorate just before serving.

6 Whip the cream until softly peaking and spoon over the two large meringues and the snail, reserving about 15ml/1 tbsp for the baby.

7 Rinse, hull and slice the strawberries and arrange a few in rings over the snail. Place the snail on a plate and add chocolate eyes and a slice from a green jelly sweet, or a little angelica, for the mouth.

8 Add some strawberries to the adult meringues, then chop or mash a few extra slices and stir them into the reserved cream for the baby. Spoon into a small dish and serve with tiny meringues.

Poached Pears

3 ripe pears

450ml/¾ pint/1⅞ cup apple juice

5ml/1 tsp powdered gelatine

few drops of green food colouring

½ small orange, rind only

½ small lemon, rind only

10ml/2 tsp chopped glacé (candied) ginger

5ml/1 tsp clear honey

5ml/1 tsp cornflour (cornstarch)

1 red liquorice bootlace

2 small currants (raisins)

1 large raisin

½ glacé (candied) cherry

1 Peel the pears, leaving the stalks in place. Cut a small circle out of the base of two pears and tunnel out the cores with a small knife.

2 Halve the remaining pear, discard the stalk, scoop out the core and then put them all in a pan with the apple juice. Bring to the boil, cover and simmer for 5 minutes, turning the pears once.

3 Lift out the pear halves and reserve, cooking the whole pears for a further 5 minutes, or until tender. Remove with a slotted spoon and place on a serving dish, reserving the cooking liquor. Finely chop one pear half and put into a small dish for the baby. Reserve the other half pear for the toddler.

4 Pour half of the reserved apple juice into a bowl, place over a pan of simmering water, add the gelatine and stir until completely dissolved. Transfer to a measuring jug (cup) and pour half over the chopped pear and chill.

5 Stir a little green colouring into the remaining gelatine mixture, pour into a shallow dish or a plate with a rim for the toddler, and chill.

6 Cut away the rind from the orange and lemon, and cut into thin strips. Add to the remaining apple juice with the ginger and honey, and simmer over a gentle heat for 5 minutes, until the rinds are soft.

7 Blend the cornflour with a little water to make a smooth paste, stir into the pan, then bring the mixture to the boil and cook, stirring until thickened. Pour over the whole pears and leave to cool.

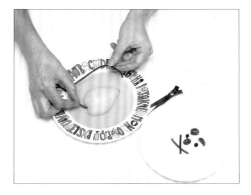

8 Place the toddler's pear, cut side down, on the green jelly (gelatine). To make a mouse, add a piece of red liquorice for a tail and two pieces for whiskers. Make two small cuts for eyes and tuck a currant into each slit. Add a large raisin for the nose. Halve the cherry and use for ears. Serve slightly chilled, with cream for the adults, if liked.

Peach Frangipane Tart

175g/6oz/1½ cups plain (all-purpose) flour

75g/3oz/6 tbsp butter

For the Filling

50g/2oz/4 tbsp butter

50g/2oz/¼ cup caster (superfine) sugar

1 egg

few drops of almond essence (extract)

50g/2oz/⅔ cup ground almonds

30ml/2 tbsp apricot jam

15ml/1 tbsp chopped glacéed (candied) peel

400g/14oz can peach slices

15ml/1 tbsp flaked (sliced) almonds

15ml/1 tbsp fromage frais or natural (plain) yogurt

icing (confectioners') sugar, for dusting

crème fraîche or natural (plain) yogurt, to serve

1 Place the flour in a bowl, cut the butter into small pieces and rub into the flour with your fingertips until the mixture resembles fine breadcrumbs.

2 Stir in 30–35ml/6–7 tsp water and mix to a smooth dough. Knead lightly on a floured surface and roll out thinly.

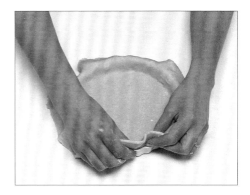

3 Lift the pastry over a rolling pin and use to line an 18cm/7in flan dish, pressing down against the sides of the dish. Trim the top.

4 Re-roll the trimmings and cut out twelve 5cm/2in circles with a fluted cookie cutter, pressing into sections of a patty tin (muffin pan). Chill the pastry for 15 minutes.

5 Preheat the oven to 190°C/ 375°F/Gas 5. Line the large flan dish with baking parchment and fill with baking beans. Cook for 10 minutes, then remove the baking beans and paper and cook the shell for a further 5 minutes.

6 Meanwhile, make the filling: cream together the butter and sugar in a bowl until light and fluffy. Beat the eggs and almond essence together, then gradually beat into the creamed sugar. Stir in the ground almonds and set aside.

7 Divide the jam among the small and large tarts, spread it into a thin layer in the large tart and sprinkle with glacéed peel. Spoon all of the almond mixture over the top and level the surface.

8 Drain the peaches and set aside three slices for the baby. Cut three slices into chunky pieces and divide among six of the small tarts, leaving six with just jam.

9 Arrange the remaining peaches over the top of the large tart and sprinkle with flaked almonds.

10 Cook the small tarts for 10 minutes and the large tart for 25 minutes, until the filling is set and browned. Dust the large tart with icing sugar and leave to cool slightly.

11 Purée the reserved peaches for the baby in a processor or liquidizer. Mix with fromage frais or yogurt and spoon into a small dish. Serve with two plain jam tarts.

12 Arrange a few fruity jam tarts on a plate for the toddler. Cut the large tart into wedges and serve with crème fraîche or natural yogurt for the adults. Test the temperature of the children's tarts before serving.

Honey and Summer Fruit Mousse

10ml/2 tsp powdered gelatine

500g/1¼lb bag frozen summer
  fruits, defrosted

20ml/4 tsp caster (superfine) sugar

500g/1¼lb tub fromage frais or
  Greek (US strained plain) yogurt

150ml/¼ pint/⅔ cup whipping
  cream

25ml/5 tsp clear honey

1 Put 30ml/2 tbsp cold water in a
cup and sprinkle the gelatine
over, making sure that all grains of
gelatine have been absorbed. Soak for
5 minutes, then heat in a pan of
simmering water until the gelatine
dissolves and the liquid is clear.
Cool slightly.

2 For the baby, process or liquidize
50g/2oz of fruit to a purée and
stir in 5ml/1 tsp sugar. Mix 45ml/3
tbsp fromage frais or yogurt with
5ml/1 tsp sugar in a separate bowl.

TIP
If you have a small novelty
mould, you may prefer to set the
toddler's portion in this rather than
a glass or plastic container.
   Make sure the gelatine isn't too
hot before adding to fromage frais
or yogurt or it may curdle.

3 Put alternate spoonfuls of
fromage frais or yogurt and
purée into a small dish for the baby.
Swirl the mixtures together with a
teaspoon. Chill until required.

4 For the toddler, process 50g/2oz
fruit with 5ml/1 tsp sugar. Mix
60ml/4 tbsp fromage frais or yogurt
with 5ml/1 tsp sugar, then stir in
10ml/2 tsp fruit purée.

5 Stir 5ml/1 tsp gelatine into the
fruit purée and 5ml/1 tsp into
the fromage frais or yogurt mixture.
Spoon the fruit mixture into the base
of a clear plastic beaker or glass and
chill until set.

6 For the adults, whip the cream
until softly peaking. Fold in the
remaining fromage frais or yogurt
and honey and add the remaining
gelatine. Pour into two 250ml/8fl oz/
1 cup moulds. Chill until set.

7 Spoon the remaining fromage
frais or yogurt mixture over the set
fruit layer in the serving glass for the
toddler and chill until set.

8 To serve, dip one of the dishes
for the adults in hot water, count
to 15, then loosen the edges with
your fingertips, invert on to a large
plate and, holding mould and plate
together, jerk to release the mousse
and remove the mould. Repeat with
the other mould. Spoon the remaining
fruits and some juice around the
desserts and serve.

NUTRITIONAL INFORMATION

The nutritional analysis below is for the whole recipe

p28 Vegetable Purées Energy 75Kcal/310kJ; Protein 2.6g; Carbohydrate 10.6g, of which sugars 10.1g; Fat 2.6g, of which saturates 1.6g; Cholesterol 8mg; Calcium 96mg; Fibre 2.4g; Sodium 51mg.

p29 Fruit Purées Energy 33Kcal/142kJ; Protein 0.7g; Carbohydrate 6.6g, of which sugars 6.6g; Fat 0.7g, of which saturates 0.4g; Cholesterol 2mg; Calcium 20mg; Fibre 1.1g; Sodium 8mg.

p34 Autumn Harvest Energy 420Kcal/1760kJ; Protein 15.4g; Carbohydrate 61.2g, of which sugars 35.7g; Fat 14g, of which saturates 8g; Cholesterol 42mg; Calcium 498mg; Fibre 11.4g; Sodium 199mg.

p35 Mixed Vegetable Platter Energy 412Kcal/1727kJ; Protein 19.3g; Carbohydrate 55.3g, of which sugars 28.5g; Fat 13.7g, of which saturates 8g; Cholesterol 42mg; Calcium 482mg; Fibre 8.6g; Sodium 190mg.

p36 Carrot, Lentil and Coriander Purée Energy 602Kcal/2531kJ; Protein 26.9g; Carbohydrate 97.5g, of which sugars 42.9g; Fat 13.9g, of which saturates 8.2g; Cholesterol 42mg; Calcium 478mg; Fibre 12.6g; Sodium 254mg.

p37 Red Pepper Risotto Energy 419Kcal/1744kJ; Protein 16g; Carbohydrate 60g, of which sugars 19.8g; Fat 12.6g, of which saturates 7.7g; Cholesterol 42mg; Calcium 409mg; Fibre 2.4g; Sodium 163mg.

p38 Parsnip and Broccoli Mix Energy 380Kcal/1590kJ; Protein 19g; Carbohydrate 43.7g, of which sugars 28g; Fat 15.2g, of which saturates 8.2g; Cholesterol 42mg; Calcium 511mg; Fibre 13.3g; Sodium 161mg.

p39 Turkey Stew with Carrots and Corn Energy 415Kcal/1756kJ; Protein 46.5g; Carbohydrate 49.2g, of which sugars 17.3g; Fat 4.9g, of which saturates 1.9g; Cholesterol 89mg; Calcium 96mg; Fibre 6.6g; Sodium 180mg.

p40 Chicken and Parsnip Purée Energy 544Kcal/2287kJ; Protein 43.8g; Carbohydrate 57.3g, of which sugars 33.5g; Fat 16.8g, of which saturates 8.6g; Cholesterol 123mg;

Calcium 503mg; Fibre 16.1g; Sodium 233mg.

p41 Cock-a-Leekie Casserole Energy 523Kcal/2204kJ; Protein 43g; Carbohydrate 59.2g, of which sugars 18.2g; Fat 14g, of which saturates 8.2g; Cholesterol 123mg; Calcium 388mg; Fibre 3.9g; Sodium 229mg.

p42 Trout and Courgette Savoury Energy 561Kcal/2352kJ; Protein 41.6g; Carbohydrate 59.8g, of which sugars 18.9g; Fat 18.5g, of which saturates 8.6g; Cholesterol 119mg; Calcium 409mg; Fibre 4.3g; Sodium 214mg.

p43 Fisherman's Pie Energy 556Kcal/2338kJ; Protein 34.8g; Carbohydrate 76.2g, of which sugars 19g; Fat 14.2g, of which saturates 8.1g; Cholesterol 83mg; Calcium 389mg; Fibre 5.1g; Sodium 222mg.

p44 Apple Ambrosia Energy 308Kcal/1285kJ; Protein 11.8g; Carbohydrate 38.8g, of which sugars 19.5g; Fat 12.1g, of which saturates 7.5g; Cholesterol 42mg; Calcium 362mg; Fibre 1.1g; Sodium 130mg.

p45 Fruit Salad Purée Energy 142Kcal/604kJ; Protein 2.8g; Carbohydrate 33.8g, of which sugars 33.8g; Fat 0.4g, of which saturates 0g; Cholesterol 0mg; Calcium 35mg; Fibre 6.6g; Sodium 8mg.

p48 Sheperd's Pie Energy 487Kcal/2045kJ; Protein 29.4g; Carbohydrate 50.1g, of which sugars 15.2g; Fat 20.1g, of which saturates 8.4g; Cholesterol 69mg; Calcium 54mg; Fibre 5.3g; Sodium 379mg.

p49 Braised Beef and Carrots Energy 466Kcal/1959kJ; Protein 43.2g; Carbohydrate 50.7g, of which sugars 22.3g; Fat 11.3g, of which saturates 4.6g; Cholesterol 110mg; Calcium 91mg; Fibre 8g; Sodium 189mg.

p50 Lamb Hotpot Energy 365Kcal/1533kJ; Protein 26.8g; Carbohydrate 34.8g, of which sugars 16.7g; Fat 14.2g, of which saturates 6.3g; Cholesterol 87mg; Calcium 118mg; Fibre 7.2g; Sodium 159mg.

p51 Lamb and Lentil Savoury Energy 332Kcal/1397kJ; Protein 29.7g; Carbohydrate 24.4g, of which sugars 10.6g; Fat 13.6g, of which saturates 6g; Cholesterol 87mg; Calcium 97mg; Fibre 3.9g; Sodium 388mg.

p52 Country Pork and Runner Beans Energy 279Kcal/1174kJ; Protein 28.7g; Carbohydrate 30g, of which sugars 11.7g; Fat 5.7g, of which saturates 1.9g; Cholesterol 73mg; Calcium 71mg; Fibre 5.6g; Sodium 122mg.

p53 Pork and Apple Savoury Energy 410Kcal/1730kJ; Protein 42.5g; Carbohydrate 44.3g, of which sugars 16.9g; Fat 8.2g, of which saturates 2.6g; Cholesterol 110mg; Calcium 132mg; Fibre 6.4g; Sodium 170mg.

p54 Nursery Kedgeree Energy 625Kcal/2604kJ; Protein 39.2g; Carbohydrate 58.5g, of which sugars 16.3g; Fat 25.9g, of which saturates 12.1g; Cholesterol 494mg; Calcium 483mg; Fibre 1.2g; Sodium 223mg.

p55 Mediterranean Vegetables Energy 284Kcal/1202kJ; Protein 12.7g; Carbohydrate 54.5g, of which sugars 25.3g; Fat 3.1g, of which saturates 0.7g; Cholesterol 0mg; Calcium 89mg; Fibre 8.3g; Sodium 362mg.

p56 Pasta with Sauce Energy 608Kcal/2537kJ; Protein 30.8g; Carbohydrate 49.2g, of which sugars 27.6g; Fat 32g, of which saturates 20g; Cholesterol 98mg; Calcium 840mg; Fibre 6.4g; Sodium 545mg.

p57 Apple and Orange Fool Energy 219Kcal/924kJ; Protein 5.5g; Carbohydrate 37.6g, of which sugars 23.8g; Fat 6.1g, of which saturates 3.8g; Cholesterol 21mg; Calcium 188mg; Fibre 2.1g; Sodium 117mg.

p58 Orchard Fruit Dessert Energy 352Kcal/1492kJ; Protein 6.9g; Carbohydrate 71g, of which sugars 57.2g; Fat 6.3g, of which saturates 3.8g; Cholesterol 21mg; Calcium 233mg; Fibre 6.9g; Sodium 122mg.

p59 Peach Melba Dessert Energy 153Kcal/650kJ; Protein 7g; Carbohydrate 30.8g, of which sugars 30.8g; Fat 1.3g, of which saturates 0.6g; Cholesterol 2mg; Calcium 238mg; Fibre 1.7g; Sodium 98mg.

p68 Lamb Couscous Energy 631Kcal/2643kJ; Protein 40.6g; Carbohydrate 67g, of which sugars 39.3g; Fat 24.1g, of which saturates 9.6g; Cholesterol 133mg; Calcium 160mg; Fibre 6.6g; Sodium 227mg.

p69 Paprika Pork Energy 533Kcal/2248kJ; Protein 50.1g; Carbohydrate 60.2g, of which sugars 17.8g; Fat

11.9g, of which saturates 3.2g; Cholesterol 110mg; Calcium 127mg; Fibre 10.7g; Sodium 659mg.

p70 Chicken and Celery Supper Energy 331Kcal/1387kJ; Protein 39.5g; Carbohydrate 24.6g, of which sugars 22.1g; Fat 8.9g, of which saturates 2g; Cholesterol 184mg; Calcium 118mg; Fibre 7.3g; Sodium 285mg.

p71 Cauliflower and Broccoli with Cheese Energy 750Kcal/ 3127kJ; Protein 45.9g; Carbohydrate 50.2g, of which sugars 22.9g; Fat 39.9g, of which saturates 24.7g; Cholesterol 115mg; Calcium 1054mg; Fibre 9.4g; Sodium 720mg.

p72 Cheese Tagliatelle with Broccoli and Ham Energy 668Kcal/2797kJ; Protein 42.9g; Carbohydrate 53.2g, of which sugars 17.4g; Fat 31.6g, of which saturates 19.3g; Cholesterol 120mg; Calcium 804mg; Fibre 4.4g; Sodium 1101mg.

p73 Baby Dhal Energy 305Kcal/1291kJ; Protein 18.1g; Carbohydrate 56.9g, of which sugars 16.6g; Fat 2g, of which saturates 0.4g; Cholesterol 0mg; Calcium 116mg; Fibre 8.8g; Sodium 59mg.

p74 Fish and Cheese Pie Energy 620Kcal/2595kJ; Protein 42.9g; Carbohydrate 49.2g, of which sugars 15.4g; Fat 27.9g, of which saturates 17.5g; Cholesterol 125mg; Calcium 701mg; Fibre 3.9g; Sodium 551mg.

p75 Fish Creole Energy 283Kcal/ 1185kJ; Protein 21.1g; Carbohydrate 46.4g, of which sugars 6.3g; Fat 1.2g, of which saturates 0.1g; Cholesterol 41mg; Calcium 43mg; Fibre 1.4g; Sodium 249mg.

p76 Chocolate Pots Energy 98Kcal/405kJ; Protein 5.8g; Carbohydrate 5.6g, of which sugars 5.5g; Fat 5.9g, of which saturates 2.8g; Cholesterol 106mg; Calcium 105mg; Fibre 0.1g; Sodium 77mg.

p77 Vanilla Custards Energy 94Kcal/392kJ; Protein 5.6g; Carbohydrate 5.5g, of which sugars 5.5g; Fat 5.7g, of which saturates 2.7g; Cholesterol 106mg; Calcium 104mg; Fibre 0g; Sodium 68mg.

p78 Marmite Bread Sticks Energy 15Kcal/63kJ; Protein 0.5g; Carbohydrate 2.4g, of which sugars 0.1g; Fat 0.4g, of which saturates 0.1g; Cholesterol 6mg; Calcium 4mg; Fibre 0.1g; Sodium 23mg.

p79 Bread Fingers with Egg Energy 14Kcal/58kJ; Protein 0.7g; Carbohydrate 1.8g, of which sugars 0.2g; Fat 0.5g, of which saturates 0.1g; Cholesterol 12mg; Calcium 8mg; Fibre 0.1g; Sodium 23mg.

p80 Cheese Straws Energy 41Kcal/172kJ; Protein 1.2g; Carbohydrate 3.3g, of which sugars 0.1g; Fat 2.6g, of which saturates 1.6g; Cholesterol 11mg; Calcium 27mg; Fibre 0.1g; Sodium 32mg.

p82 Mini Cup Cakes Energy 31Kcal/130kJ; Protein 0.4g; Carbohydrate 3.5g, of which sugars 2.1g; Fat 1.8g, of which saturates 0.1g; Cholesterol 7mg; Calcium 9mg; Fibre 0.1g; Sodium 25mg.

p83 Shortbread Shapes Energy 28Kcal/117kJ; Protein 0.3g; Carbohydrate 3.2g, of which sugars 0.9g; Fat 1.7g, of which saturates 1g; Cholesterol 4mg; Calcium 4mg; Fibre 0.1g; Sodium 12mg.

p92 Sticky Chicken Energy 109Kcal/458kJ; Protein 14.7g; Carbohydrate 1.2g, of which sugars 1.1g; Fat 5.1g, of which saturates 1.4g; Cholesterol 77mg; Calcium 9mg; Fibre 0g; Sodium 222mg.

p94 Coriander Chicken Casserole Energy 157Kcal/658kJ; Protein 21.8g; Carbohydrate 7.6g, of which sugars 4.8g; Fat 4.6g, of which saturates 1g; Cholesterol 105mg; Calcium 38mg; Fibre 1.6g; Sodium 101mg.

p94 Chicken and Cheese Parcels Energy 252Kcal/1050kJ; Protein 27.6g; Carbohydrate 0.2g, of which sugars 0.2g; Fat 15.1g, of which saturates 6.5g; Cholesterol 87mg; Calcium 190mg; Fibre 0g; Sodium 436mg.

p96 Peppered Beef Casserole Energy 229Kcal/958kJ; Protein 18g; Carbohydrate 26.5g, of which sugars 8.2g; Fat 6.3g, of which saturates 2.3g; Cholesterol 33mg; Calcium 43mg; Fibre 3.3g; Sodium 251mg.

p 97 Lamb Stew Energy 152Kcal/635kJ; Protein 12.3g; Carbohydrate 7.5g, of which sugars 5g; Fat 8.4g, of which saturates 3.3g; Cholesterol 44mg; Calcium 29mg; Fibre 2.2g; Sodium 59mg.

p98 Mexican Beef Energy 171Kcal/715kJ; Protein 9.5g; Carbohydrate 11.8g, of which sugars 2.9g; Fat 9.8g, of which saturates

3.9g; Cholesterol 23mg; Calcium 83mg; Fibre 1.7g; Sodium 275mg.

p98 Lamb and Celery Casserole Energy 142Kcal/596kJ; Protein 12.6g; Carbohydrate 8.4g, of which sugars 3.8g; Fat 6.8g, of which saturates 3.1g; Cholesterol 44mg; Calcium 33mg; Fibre 1.5g; Sodium 67mg.

p100 Shepherd's Pie Energy 388Kcal/1617kJ; Protein 21.7g; Carbohydrate 28.7g, of which sugars 11.9g; Fat 21.5g, of which saturates 10.3g; Cholesterol 69mg; Calcium 69mg; Fibre 4.5g; Sodium 382mg.

p101 Tuna Fish Cakes Energy 263Kcal/1104kJ; Protein 16.6g; Carbohydrate 19.4g, of which sugars 4.9g; Fat 13.9g, of which saturates 1.7g; Cholesterol 81mg; Calcium 80mg; Fibre 3.3g; Sodium 183mg.

p102 Fish and Cheese Pies Energy 300Kcal/1258kJ; Protein 19.3g; Carbohydrate 25.5g, of which sugars 6.5g; Fat 13.9g, of which saturates 7.8g; Cholesterol 59mg; Calcium 228mg; Fibre 1.6g; Sodium 246mg.

p103 Surprise Fish Parcels Energy 89Kcal/376kJ; Protein 17.9g; Carbohydrate 2.5g, of which sugars 2.4g; Fat 0.9g, of which saturates 0.2g; Cholesterol 32mg; Calcium 36mg; Fibre 1g; Sodium 670mg.

p104 Cowboy Sausages and Beans Energy 225Kcal/944kJ; Protein 9.8g; Carbohydrate 22.7g, of which sugars 8.4g; Fat 11.4g, of which saturates 4.1g; Cholesterol 15mg; Calcium 89mg; Fibre 5.4g; Sodium 702mg.

p104 Mini Toad in the Hole Energy 282Kcal/1183kJ; Protein 11.5g; Carbohydrate 28.3g, of which sugars 2.9g; Fat 14.6g, of which saturates 4.8g; Cholesterol 119mg; Calcium 131mg; Fibre 1.3g; Sodium 372mg.

p106 Pork Hotpot Energy 230Kcal/967kJ; Protein 21.4g; Carbohydrate 24.7g, of which sugars 7.4g; Fat 5.7g, of which saturates 1.6g; Cholesterol 55mg; Calcium 32mg; Fibre 2.5g; Sodium 134mg.

p107 Pork and Lentil Casserole Energy 369Kcal/1531kJ; Protein 17.7g; Carbohydrate 12.8g, of which sugars 5.2g; Fat 27.8g, of which saturates 9.9g; Cholesterol 63mg; Calcium 31mg; Fibre 2.1g; Sodium 65mg.

p108 Sticky Ribs and Apple Slaw Energy 454Kcal/1896kJ; Protein 23g; Carbohydrate 25.2g, of which sugars 16.4g; Fat 29.8g, of which saturates 8g; Cholesterol 86mg; Calcium 44mg; Fibre 2.1g; Sodium 357mg.

p109 Mini Cheese and Ham Tarts Energy 100Kcal/419kJ; Protein 3.2g; Carbohydrate 9.6g, of which sugars 1.3g; Fat 5.6g, of which saturates 1.2g; Cholesterol 21mg; Calcium 59mg; Fibre 0.4g; Sodium 101mg.

p110 Pick-up Sticks Energy 54Kcal/223kJ; Protein 1.7g; Carbohydrate 7.7g, of which sugars 6.9g; Fat 2g, of which saturates 0.3g; Cholesterol 0mg; Calcium 29mg; Fibre 2.3g; Sodium 318mg.

p112 Spinach Pancakes with Ham and Cheese Energy 265Kcal/1111kJ; Protein 11.7g; Carbohydrate 22g, of which sugars 5.5g; Fat 15g, of which saturates 5g; Cholesterol 89mg; Calcium 250mg; Fibre 1.2g; Sodium 325mg.

p113 Cauliflower and Broccoli with Cheese Energy 264Kcal/1101kJ; Protein 14.6g; Carbohydrate 11.9g, of which sugars 5.9g; Fat 17.6g, of which saturates 6.1g; Cholesterol 119mg; Calcium 293mg; Fibre 2.1g; Sodium 281mg.

p114 Potato Boats Energy 257Kcal/1073kJ; Protein 10.9g; Carbohydrate 24.7g, of which sugars 7.4g; Fat 13.4g, of which saturates 6.4g; Cholesterol 39mg; Calcium 165mg; Fibre 2.9g; Sodium 573mg.

p115 Fat Cats Energy 553Kcal/2308kJ; Protein 13.5g; Carbohydrate 46.6g, of which sugars 4.7g; Fat 36.8g, of which saturates 3.9g; Cholesterol 18mg; Calcium 258mg; Fibre 0.9g; Sodium 514mg.

p116 Potato, Carrot and Courgette Rosti Energy 37Kcal/155kJ; Protein 0.7g; Carbohydrate 5.2g, of which sugars 1g; Fat 1.6g, of which saturates 0.2g; Cholesterol 0mg; Calcium 5mg; Fibre 0.5g; Sodium 5mg.

p116 Veggie Burgers Energy 118Kcal/495kJ; Protein 4.1g; Carbohydrate 13.3g, of which sugars 2g; Fat 5.8g, of which saturates 1.7g; Cholesterol 54mg; Calcium 68mg; Fibre 1.4g; Sodium 54mg.

p118 Vegetable Lasagne Energy 296Kcal/1243kJ; Protein 11.7g;

Carbohydrate 30.7g, of which sugars 8.6g; Fat 14.5g, of which saturates 8g; Cholesterol 33mg; Calcium 243mg; Fibre 2.9g; Sodium 210mg.

p119 Aubergine Bolognaise Energy 184Kcal/781kJ; Protein 8.2g; Carbohydrate 36.6g, of which sugars 9.6g; Fat 1.5g, of which saturates 0.4g; Cholesterol 0mg; Calcium 39mg; Fibre 4.9g; Sodium 58mg.

p120 Speedy Chicken Pie Energy 244Kcal/1015kJ; Protein 14.9g; Carbohydrate 7.5g, of which sugars 1.6g; Fat 17.2g, of which saturates 4.6g; Cholesterol 54mg; Calcium 68mg; Fibre 0.7g; Sodium 241mg.

p122 Skinny Dippers Energy 444Kcal/1870kJ; Protein 33.4g; Carbohydrate 45.9g, of which sugars 10g; Fat 15.1g, of which saturates 8.2g; Cholesterol 99mg; Calcium 160mg; Fibre 3g; Sodium 771mg.

p123 Sweet and Sour Chicken Energy 338Kcal/1409kJ; Protein 19.3g; Carbohydrate 29g, of which sugars 6.5g; Fat 16.3g, of which saturates 4.1g; Cholesterol 170mg; Calcium 53mg; Fibre 0.9g; Sodium 351mg.

p124 Ham and Tomato Scramble Energy 192Kcal/808kJ; Protein 15.7g; Carbohydrate 16.7g, of which sugars 4g; Fat 7.6g, of which saturates 2.1g; Cholesterol 211mg; Calcium 74mg; Fibre 1.2g; Sodium 638mg.

p124 Ham Salad Clown Energy 94Kcal/391kJ; Protein 8.5g; Carbohydrate 2.2g, of which sugars 2.2g; Fat 5.5g, of which saturates 3.2g; Cholesterol 46mg; Calcium 99mg; Fibre 0.2g; Sodium 398mg.

p126 Spanish Omelette Energy 130Kcal/546kJ; Protein 9.3g; Carbohydrate 9.9g, of which sugars 1.8g; Fat 6.4g, of which saturates 1.7g; Cholesterol 110mg; Calcium 22mg; Fibre 1.2g; Sodium 349mg.

p127 Pasta with Ham Sauce
Energy 434Kcal/1814kJ; Protein 20g; Carbohydrate 37g, of which sugars 5.6g; Fat 23.6g, of which saturates 6.7g; Cholesterol 43mg; Calcium 310mg; Fibre 2.4g; Sodium 635mg.

p128 Quickie Kebabs Energy 59Kcal/248kJ; Protein 5.2g; Carbohydrate 3g, of which sugars 2.9g; Fat 3g, of which saturates 0.6g; Cholesterol 15mg; Calcium 6mg; Fibre 0.6g; Sodium 358mg.

p128 Sausage Wrappers Energy 272Kcal/1136kJ; Protein 20.4g; Carbohydrate 7.8g, of which sugars 2.8g; Fat 18g, of which saturates 5.7g; Cholesterol 137mg; Calcium 24mg; Fibre 0.8g; Sodium 1342mg.

p130 Corned Beef Hash Energy 222Kcal/931kJ; Protein 16.9g; Carbohydrate 18.1g, of which sugars 5g; Fat 9.6g, of which saturates 3.7g; Cholesterol 48mg; Calcium 34mg; Fibre 1.5g; Sodium 628mg.

p131 Cannibal Necklaces Energy 240Kcal/1003kJ; Protein 14.1g; Carbohydrate 19.5g, of which sugars 5.2g; Fat 12.2g, of which saturates 4.8g; Cholesterol 36mg; Calcium 231mg; Fibre 2.3g; Sodium 383mg.

p132 Beef Burgers Energy 305Kcal/ 1282kJ; Protein 16.3g; Carbohydrate 34.1g, of which sugars 4g; Fat 12.5g, of which saturates 5.1g; Cholesterol 35mg; Calcium 53mg; Fibre 2.5g; Sodium 222mg.

p133 Four Fast Fishes Energy 268Kcal/1124kJ; Protein 16.4g; Carbohydrate 27.1g, of which sugars 3.8g; Fat 11.2g, of which saturates 1.6g; Cholesterol 48mg; Calcium 99mg; Fibre 2.3g; Sodium 306mg.

p134 Tuna Risotto Energy 190Kcal/798kJ; Protein 15.8g; Carbohydrate 26.6g, of which sugars 3.7g; Fat 2.4g, of which saturates 0.4g; Cholesterol 26mg; Calcium 22mg; Fibre 1.7g; Sodium 243mg.

p134 Fish Finger Log Cabins Energy 99Kcal/414kJ; Protein 6.4g; Carbohydrate 9.3g, of which sugars 2.3g; Fat 4.3g, of which saturates 1.3g; Cholesterol 15mg; Calcium 81mg; Fibre 1.1g; Sodium 172mg.

p136 Shape Sorters Energy 300Kcal/1250kJ; Protein 12.2g; Carbohydrate 16.2g, of which sugars 2.6g; Fat 20.6g, of which saturates 7.4g; Cholesterol 24mg; Calcium 223mg; Fibre 1.5g; Sodium 416mg.

p136 Happy Families Energy 251Kcal/1051kJ; Protein 13.4g; Carbohydrate 22.2g, of which sugars 4.6g; Fat 12.7g, of which saturates 4.6g; Cholesterol 40mg; Calcium 229mg; Fibre 1.1g; Sodium 942mg.

p138 French Toast Butterflies Energy 243Kcal/1018kJ; Protein 17.2g; Carbohydrate 17g, of which sugars 3.9g; Fat 12g, of which saturates 5.2g; Cholesterol 127mg; Calcium 216mg; Fibre 2.4g; Sodium 615mg.

p139 Tuna Flowers Energy 384Kcal/1607kJ; Protein 17.4g; Carbohydrate 31.8g, of which sugars 4.3g; Fat 21.3g, of which saturates 11.6g; Cholesterol 63mg; Calcium 251mg; Fibre 2g; Sodium 600mg.

p140 Noughts and Crosses Energy 379Kcal/1578kJ; Protein 20.5g; Carbohydrate 15.4g, of which sugars 2.6g; Fat 25.4g, of which saturates 14.7g; Cholesterol 68mg; Calcium 462mg; Fibre 1.1g; Sodium 827mg.

p140 Cheese Strips on Toast Energy 273Kcal/1137kJ; Protein 15g; Carbohydrate 13.5g, of which sugars 0.9g; Fat 16.9g, of which saturates 10.9g; Cholesterol 49mg; Calcium 400mg; Fibre 0.5g; Sodium 503mg.

p142 Speedy Sausage Rolls Energy 91Kcal/378kJ; Protein 2.3g; Carbohydrate 7.1g, of which sugars 0.5g; Fat 6.1g, of which saturates 2.7g; Cholesterol 11mg; Calcium 19mg; Fibre 0.2g; Sodium 171mg.

p143 Pizza Clock Energy 204Kcal/856kJ; Protein 10g; Carbohydrate 23.2g, of which sugars 9.3g; Fat 8.1g, of which saturates 4.3g; Cholesterol 25mg; Calcium 173mg; Fibre 2.2g; Sodium 547mg.

p144 Spotted Sandwiches Energy 275Kcal/1151kJ; Protein 8.1g; Carbohydrate 28.2g, of which sugars 3.8g; Fat 15.3g, of which saturates 2.7g; Cholesterol 106mg; Calcium 107mg; Fibre 2.1g; Sodium 382mg.

p144 Sandwich Snails Energy 188Kcal/783kJ; Protein 6.6g; Carbohydrate 11.6g, of which sugars 2.9g; Fat 12.9g, of which saturates 4.6g; Cholesterol 24mg; Calcium 124mg; Fibre 0.8g; Sodium 345mg.

p146 Fruit Fondue Energy 197Kcal/833kJ; Protein 3.8g; Carbohydrate 33.7g, of which sugars 30.2g; Fat 5.4g, of which saturates 2.4g; Cholesterol 4mg; Calcium 107mg; Fibre 1.5g; Sodium 44mg.

p148 Strawberry Ice Cream Energy 2026Kcal/8391kJ; Protein 19.9g; Carbohydrate 101.4g, of which sugars 86.5g; Fat 169.2g, of which saturates 100.2g; Cholesterol 420mg; Calcium 606mg; Fibre 5.4g; Sodium 267mg.

p149 Raspberry Sorbet Energy 1055Kcal/4518kJ; Protein 10.6g; Carbohydrate 266.2g, of which sugars 266.2g; Fat 2g, of which saturates 0.7g; Cholesterol 0mg; Calcium 288mg; Fibre 16.9g; Sodium 34mg.

p150 Yogurt Lollies Energy 41Kcal/ 172kJ; Protein 1.9g; Carbohydrate 7.3g, of which sugars 7.3g; Fat 0.6g, of which saturates 0.4g; Cholesterol 2mg; Calcium 68mg; Fibre 0g; Sodium 27mg.

p150 Jolly Jellies Energy 195Kcal/ 824kJ; Protein 4.9g; Carbohydrate 39.2g, of which sugars 38.9g; Fat 3.2g, of which saturates 2g; Cholesterol 9mg; Calcium 55mg; Fibre 0.3g; Sodium 26mg.

p152 Pancakes Energy 285Kcal/ 1194kJ; Protein 8.1g; Carbohydrate 33.3g, of which sugars 19.9g; Fat 14.2g, of which saturates 6.1g; Cholesterol 66mg; Calcium 163mg; Fibre 1.5g; Sodium 78mg.

p153 Traffic Light Sundaes Energy 224Kcal/940kJ; Protein 4.3g; Carbohydrate 36.7g, of which sugars 36.6g; Fat 7.7g, of which saturates 4.5g; Cholesterol 0mg; Calcium 73mg; Fibre 0.5g; Sodium 41mg.

p154 Cheat's Trifle Energy 175Kcal/741kJ; Protein 4.7g; Carbohydrate 32.5g, of which sugars 26.2g; Fat 3.1g, of which saturates 0.3g; Cholesterol 2mg; Calcium 115mg; Fibre 0.9g; Sodium 73mg.

p154 Baked Bananas Energy 184Kcal/770kJ; Protein 2.9g; Carbohydrate 27g, of which sugars 25.1g; Fat 7.8g, of which saturates 4.6g; Cholesterol 0mg; Calcium 55mg; Fibre 0.9g; Sodium 31mg.

p156 Orange and Apple Rockies Energy 87Kcal/366kJ; Protein 1.3g; Carbohydrate 11.6g, of which sugars 4.5g; Fat 4.3g, of which saturates 0.9g; Cholesterol 8mg; Calcium 19mg; Fibre 0.5g; Sodium 42mg.

p158 Date Crunch Energy 120Kcal/503kJ; Protein 1.3g; Carbohydrate 15.3g, of which sugars 10.1g; Fat 6.4g, of which saturates 3.6g; Cholesterol 12mg; Calcium 27mg; Fibre 0.4g; Sodium 85mg.

p159 Chocolate Dominoes Energy 335Kcal/1400kJ; Protein 2.9g; Carbohydrate 38.8g, of which sugars 31.3g; Fat 19.8g, of which saturates 6.4g; Cholesterol 59mg; Calcium 41mg; Fibre 0.7g; Sodium 199mg.

p160 Marshmallow Krispie Cakes Energy 56Kcal/235kJ; Protein 0.7g; Carbohydrate 9g, of which sugars 4.4g; Fat 2.2g, of which saturates 1.1g; Cholesterol 3mg; Calcium 39mg; Fibre 0g; Sodium 28mg.

p160 Mini-muffins Energy 67Kcal/281kJ; Protein 1.4g; Carbohydrate 11.1g, of which sugars 4.8g; Fat 2.2g, of which saturates 1.2g; Cholesterol 13mg; Calcium 25mg; Fibre 0.4g; Sodium 19mg.

p162 Cup Cake Faces Energy 328Kcal/1374kJ; Protein 3.2g; Carbohydrate 42.5g, of which sugars 33.1g; Fat 17.3g, of which saturates 5.4g; Cholesterol 43mg; Calcium 53mg; Fibre 0.6g; Sodium 127mg.

p163 Gingerbread People Energy 94Kcal/395kJ; Protein 1.2g; Carbohydrate 16.5g, of which sugars 9.3g; Fat 3g, of which saturates 0.7g; Cholesterol 0mg; Calcium 19mg; Fibre 0.4g; Sodium 23mg.

p164 Bread Animals Energy 147Kcal/624kJ; Protein 4.7g; Carbohydrate 28.5g, of which sugars 1.8g; Fat 2.4g, of which saturates 0.4g; Cholesterol 13mg; Calcium 55mg; Fibre 1.4g; Sodium 139mg.

p166 Cheese Shapes Energy 184Kcal/769kJ; Protein 5.2g; Carbohydrate 18.2g, of which sugars 0.4g; Fat 10.4g, of which saturates 2g; Cholesterol 33mg; Calcium 100mg; Fibre 0.8g; Sodium 127mg.

p169 Marmite and Cheese Whirls Energy 76Kcal/318kJ; Protein 2.1g; Carbohydrate 5.8g, of which sugars 0.2g; Fat 5.2g, of which saturates 0.8g; Cholesterol 15mg; Calcium 34mg; Fibre 0g; Sodium 82mg.

p174 Mediterranean Lamb Energy 1547Kcal/6457kJ; Protein 103.4g; Carbohydrate 63.3g, of which sugars 43g; Fat 99.8g, of which saturates 42.2g; Cholesterol 333mg; Calcium 281mg; Fibre 16.5g; Sodium 951mg.

p176 Lamb Hotpot Energy 1217Kcal/5100kJ; Protein 85.2g; Carbohydrate 90.6g, of which sugars 34.3g; Fat 59.6g, of which saturates 27.4g; Cholesterol 298mg; Calcium 256mg; Fibre 19.5g; Sodium 484mg.

p178 Beef Korma Energy 1034Kcal/4318kJ; Protein 78.6g; Carbohydrate 48.5g, of which sugars 28.9g; Fat 59.7g, of which saturates 25.2g; Cholesterol 210mg; Calcium 222mg; Fibre 9g; Sodium 542mg.

p180 Bobotie with Baked Potatoes and Broccoli Energy 2005Kcal/8426kJ; Protein 126.5g; Carbohydrate 213.8g, of which sugars 70.5g; Fat 77.7g, of which saturates 30.4g; Cholesterol 598mg; Calcium 593mg; Fibre 30.8g; Sodium 1611mg.

p182 Moussaka Energy 1805Kcal/7551kJ; Protein 98.9g; Carbohydrate 121.8g, of which sugars 37.6g; Fat 106.1g, of which saturates 46.8g; Cholesterol 360mg; Calcium 684mg; Fibre 15g; Sodium 903mg.

p184 Chilli Con Carne Energy 2113Kcal/8830kJ; Protein 125.5g; Carbohydrate 155.4g, of which sugars 46.9g; Fat 114g, of which saturates 44.6g; Cholesterol 297mg; Calcium 387mg; Fibre 29.1g; Sodium 1374mg.

p186 Beef Bourguignon with Creamed Potatoes Energy 1690Kcal/7073kJ; Protein 121.4g; Carbohydrate 118.8g, of which sugars 26.2g; Fat 77.2g, of which saturates 32.7g; Cholesterol 318mg; Calcium 303mg; Fibre 12.3g; Sodium 584mg.

p188 Osso Bucco Pork with Rice Energy 2089Kcal/8726kJ; Protein 187.1g; Carbohydrate 149g, of which sugars 26.4g; Fat 82.3g, of which saturates 30.5g; Cholesterol 591mg; Calcium 449mg; Fibre 10.4g; Sodium 797mg.

p190 Pork Stir Fry Energy 807Kcal/3377kJ; Protein 73.5g; Carbohydrate 58.8g, of which sugars 40.8g; Fat 32.2g, of which saturates 9g; Cholesterol 158mg; Calcium 163mg; Fibre 12.3g; Sodium 1458mg.

p192 Sausage Casserole Energy 2486Kcal/10416kJ; Protein 85.3g; Carbohydrate 272.4g, of which sugars 68.3g; Fat 124.7g, of which saturates 47.6g; Cholesterol 180mg; Calcium 641mg; Fibre 40.2g; Sodium 5366mg.

p194 Chicken and Thyme Casserole Energy 1320Kcal/5552kJ; Protein 147.1g; Carbohydrate 107.9g, of which sugars 20.9g; Fat 36.2g, of which saturates 10.5g; Cholesterol 635mg; Calcium 235mg; Fibre 13.1g; Sodium 629mg.

p196 Tandoori-style Chicken Energy 1209Kcal/5080kJ; Protein 116.5g; Carbohydrate 68.6g, of which sugars 16.8g; Fat 54.1g, of which saturates 13g; Cholesterol 522mg; Calcium 401mg; Fibre 4.5g; Sodium 377mg.

p198 Chicken Wrappers Energy 1472Kcal/6187kJ; Protein 175g; Carbohydrate 72.7g, of which sugars 11.7g; Fat 54.3g, of which saturates 24.2g; Cholesterol 527mg; Calcium 512mg; Fibre 8.8g; Sodium 1451mg.

p200 Pan-fried Turkey with Coriander Energy 1568Kcal/6566kJ; Protein 122.9g; Carbohydrate 151g, of which sugars 20.5g; Fat 52.5g, of which saturates 33g; Cholesterol 222mg; Calcium 92mg; Fibre 4.2g; Sodium 375mg.

p202 Chicken Salad Energy 1058Kcal/4461kJ; Protein 119.4g; Carbohydrate 76.6g, of which sugars 22.4g; Fat 32.7g, of which saturates 17.6g; Cholesterol 379mg; Calcium 224mg; Fibre 7.3g; Sodium 995mg.

p204 Paella Energy 1212Kcal/5080kJ; Protein 112.9g; Carbohydrate 149.1g, of which sugars 22.9g; Fat 17.9g, of which saturates 2.6g; Cholesterol 408mg; Calcium 271mg; Fibre 9.7g; Sodium 498mg.

p206 Fish Cakes Energy 1349Kcal/5672kJ; Protein 110.3g; Carbohydrate 137.4g, of which sugars 30.6g; Fat 43.2g, of which saturates 21.9g; Cholesterol 287mg; Calcium 595mg; Fibre 13.2g; Sodium 2315mg.

p208 Fishy Vol-au-Vents Energy 1690Kcal/7071kJ; Protein 98.5g; Carbohydrate 128.3g, of which sugars 15.5g; Fat 93g, of which saturates 18.3g; Cholesterol 334mg; Calcium 527mg; Fibre 3.1g; Sodium 1351mg.

p210 Salmon and Cod Kebabs Energy 1636Kcal/6823kJ; Protein 114g; Carbohydrate 94.6g, of which sugars 24.7g; Fat 91.6g, of which saturates 34.7g; Cholesterol 349mg; Calcium 195mg; Fibre 16.4g; Sodium 724mg.

p212 Tuna Florentine Energy 2325Kcal/9709kJ; Protein 164.5g; Carbohydrate 95.1g, of which sugars 20.8g; Fat 139.5g, of which saturates 72.3g; Cholesterol 791mg; Calcium 3035mg; Fibre 8.9g; Sodium 3526mg.

p214 Cheese on Toast Energy 1456Kcal/6064kJ; Protein 72g; Carbohydrate 56.1g, of which sugars

3.7g; Fat 102.1g, of which saturates 56.8g; Cholesterol 266mg; Calcium 1644mg; Fibre 3.1g; Sodium 4100mg.

p216 Penne with Tomato Sauce Energy 1027Kcal/4327kJ; Protein 38.8g; Carbohydrate 144.3g, of which sugars 36.2g; Fat 35.4g, of which saturates 15.5g; Cholesterol 58mg; Calcium 565mg; Fibre 12.7g; Sodium 519mg.

p218 Courgette Gougère Energy 1456Kcal/6051kJ; Protein 58.8g; Carbohydrate 69.4g, of which sugars 17.9g; Fat 104.4g, of which saturates 56.5g; Cholesterol 599mg; Calcium 1132mg; Fibre 9.5g; Sodium 1308mg.

p220 Cheese Vegetable Crumble Energy 2051Kcal/8546kJ; Protein 79.8g; Carbohydrate 146.4g, of which sugars 53g; Fat 128.7g, of which saturates 31.5g; Cholesterol 112mg; Calcium 1678mg; Fibre 46.4g; Sodium 2221mg.

p222 Vegetable Tagine Energy 1141Kcal/4800kJ; Protein 44.4g; Carbohydrate 190.4g, of which sugars 61.5g; Fat 27.5g, of which saturates 3.3g; Cholesterol 0mg; Calcium 444mg; Fibre 33.7g; Sodium 1071mg.

p224 Stilton and Leek Tart Energy 2221Kcal/9261kJ; Protein 81.2g; Carbohydrate 154.7g, of which sugars 20.1g; Fat 145.1g, of which saturates 85.6g; Cholesterol 933mg; Calcium 1148mg; Fibre 9.8g; Sodium 2398mg.

p226 Bread and Butter Pudding Energy 1528Kcal/6452kJ; Protein 57.5g; Carbohydrate 214.2g, of which sugars 126g; Fat 52.3g, of which saturates 22.4g; Cholesterol 832mg; Calcium 821mg; Fibre 11.3g; Sodium 1573mg.

p228 Eve's Pudding Energy 1198Kcal/5049kJ; Protein 13.7g; Carbohydrate 190.7g, of which sugars 152.6g; Fat 47.9g, of which saturates 27.7g; Cholesterol 297mg; Calcium 201mg; Fibre 11.1g; Sodium 392mg.

p230 Orange and Strawberry Shortcakes Energy 1054Kcal/4407kJ; Protein 20.7g; Carbohydrate 118.9g, of which sugars 61.7g; Fat 60.2g, of which saturates 35.3g; Cholesterol 107mg; Calcium 438mg; Fibre 5.1g; Sodium 447mg.

p232 Exotic Fruit Brûlée Energy 700Kcal/2940kJ; Protein 24.7g; Carbohydrate 82.4g, of which sugars 81.8g; Fat 36.4g, of which saturates

18.4g; Cholesterol 0mg; Calcium 584mg; Fibre 5.5g; Sodium 259mg.

p234 Plum Crumble Energy 1644Kcal/6930kJ; Protein 28g; Carbohydrate 256.1g, of which sugars 145.8g; Fat 63.7g, of which saturates 23.2g; Cholesterol 85mg; Calcium 391mg; Fibre 16.4g; Sodium 287mg.

p236 Chocolate and Orange Trifle Energy 1385Kcal/5790kJ; Protein 16.7g; Carbohydrate 139.1g, of which sugars 115.9g; Fat 80.5g, of which saturates 43.7g; Cholesterol 197mg; Calcium 441mg; Fibre 3.5g; Sodium 418mg.

p238 Apple Strudel Energy 1189Kcal/5023kJ; Protein 20.6g; Carbohydrate 200.8g, of which sugars 123.8g; Fat 39.5g, of which saturates 14.6g; Cholesterol 53mg; Calcium 316mg; Fibre 16.6g; Sodium 185mg.

p240 Strawberry Pavlova Energy 1288Kcal/5375kJ; Protein 10.7g; Carbohydrate 137.7g, of which sugars 137.7g; Fat 80.8g, of which saturates 50.1g; Cholesterol 206mg; Calcium 178mg; Fibre 2.8g; Sodium 177mg.

p242 Poached Pears Energy 374Kcal/1597kJ; Protein 1.8g; Carbohydrate 95.7g, of which sugars 95.7g; Fat 0.9g, of which saturates 0g; Cholesterol 0mg; Calcium 81mg; Fibre 9.9g; Sodium 23mg.

p244 Peach Frangipane Tart Energy 2481Kcal/10368kJ; Protein 40.9g; Carbohydrate 262.6g, of which sugars 127.4g; Fat 148.2g, of which saturates 70.7g; Cholesterol 458mg; Calcium 534mg; Fibre 14.2g; Sodium 954mg.

p246 Honey and Summer Fruit Mousse Energy 1350Kcal/5603kJ; Protein 37.6g; Carbohydrate 76.9g, of which sugars 75.4g; Fat 101g, of which saturates 65.5g; Cholesterol 201mg; Calcium 728mg; Fibre 5.5g; Sodium 249mg.

INDEX

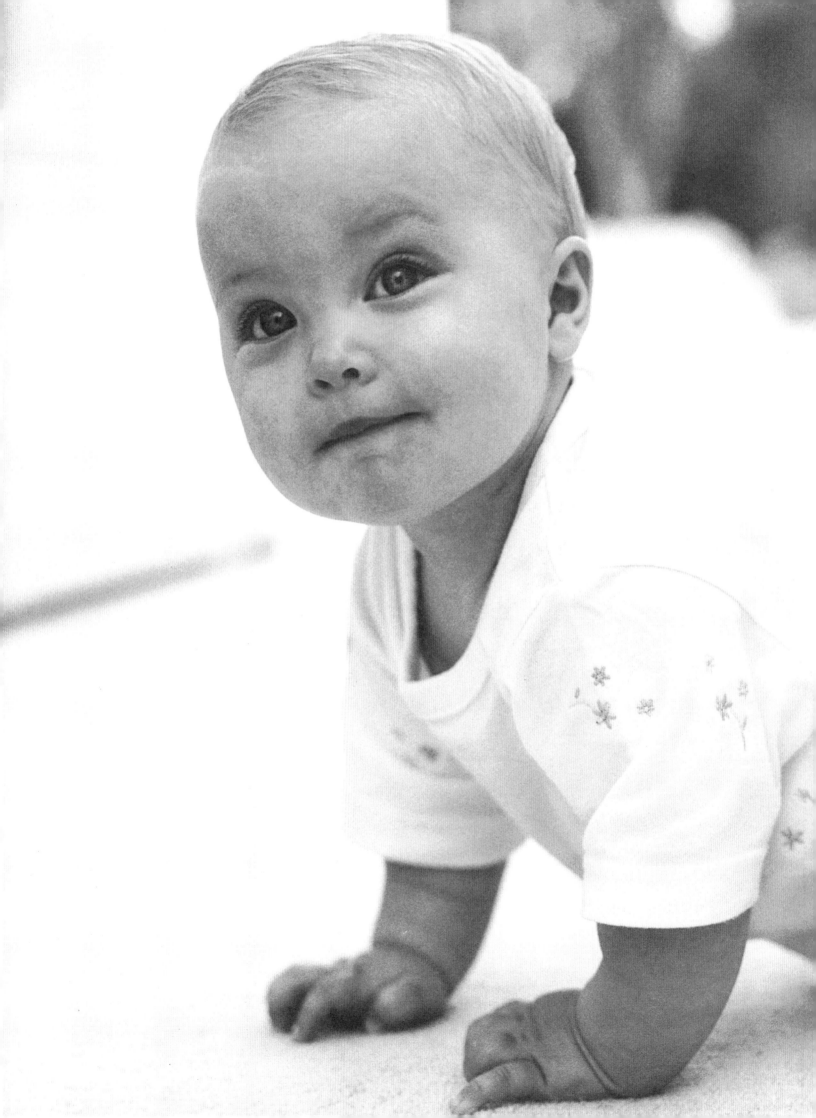